The Expansion Code

Success Rewired From the Inside Out

Kayla Burch

KaylaBurch

ISBN: 979-8-9986384-0-4

Cover art and design by Coltyn Harrill
This book is a work of nonfiction. While every effort has been made to ensure the accuracy and completeness of the information contained herein, the author assumes no responsibility for errors, inaccuracies, omissions, or any outcomes from the use of this information.

Trigger Response Method™ and **The Expansion Code™** are proprietary methods created by Kayla Burch. All trademarks, registered trademarks, and service marks mentioned are the property of their respective owners.

First Edition, 2025
Printed in the United States of America

For more information, visit:
www.kaylaburch.com

To MaKenzie, Maxx, Maverick, and Maebri—

You are my greatest expansion and most sacred blessings.
This journey, this book, and everything I am... began
with you.

Contents

Introduction

When Success Isn't Safe

There's a specific kind of fear that high performers carry. It doesn't show up in your first year or when you're just getting started. It creeps in when you're already succeeding.

When things look solid from the outside. When the clients are renewing. The praise is coming in. The results speak for themselves. And still—something inside you whispers: *It's not enough.*

That was me.

I was working as one of the top coaches at a high-level company—mentoring others, leading trainings, being trusted to shape the next generation of leaders. On paper, I had made it.

And yet, I was still waiting for the shoe to drop.

I remember staring at my glowing screen, reading another email from a client raving about their results—and instead of celebrating, I braced myself.

What if they find out I'm not actually that good?

I knew how to smile on camera. I knew how to lead the group, run the call, deliver the value. But the moment I logged off, the pressure would come rushing back.

Did I say enough?

Did I say too much?

Is this the moment they realize I'm not who they think I am?

That's the exhausting part. It's not the work. It's who you think you have to be to hold it.

It didn't matter how many people I helped or how much I had accomplished. The internal story hadn't caught up. I was still being run by an outdated identity—one that said success wasn't safe, ease wasn't earned, and I wasn't the kind of person who was meant for either.

That was the hidden pattern running the show. Even though I had outgrown the version of myself that once doubted my intelligence, my worth, and my ability to succeed, the story hadn't updated. It was still operating in the background, shaping my reality, keeping me stuck in a loop where success never felt safe.

And this—this is where so many high achievers get caught.

You build, you achieve, you check off all the boxes. You get the praise, the promotions, the proof that you're good enough. But something inside you still doesn't believe it. And because you don't believe it, you can't fully receive it. Instead, you keep running, trying to outrun a feeling that won't go away.

At first, you assume you just need to accomplish more. Maybe once you hit the next milestone, the feeling will go away. Maybe if you get the next opportunity, the next big client, the next level of income, then you'll finally feel safe in your success.

But it never works.

Because the part of you that still doesn't believe you're enough?

It doesn't care about external proof. It will always find a way to discount it, dismiss it, or demand more before you're allowed to rest.

That's why you see wildly successful people—people who have built multimillion-dollar businesses, people who lead massive teams, people who seem like they should have it all—still feel like it's never enough.

That's why people with thousands of clients, best-selling books, public recognition—still feel like frauds.

Because success isn't just about what you accomplish. It's about whether your internal identity can hold it.

The Hustle Behind the Mask

I see it all the time—the entrepreneurs who are addicted to growth, but terrified of slowing down long enough to actually enjoy it.

The ones who can't take a breath between launches because they're afraid the whole thing will collapse if they do.

The ones who tell themselves they'll rest once they hit the next goal, but by the time they get there, the finish line has already moved.

The ones who have achieved more than they ever thought possible—yet still wake up feeling like they're behind.

They tell themselves it's just ambition. The hunger that got them here.

But the truth?

It's fear.

Fear that if they stop—even for a moment—everything they've built will slip through their fingers.

Fear that if they slow down, they'll lose momentum, get left behind, or suddenly become irrelevant.

Fear that if they're not constantly proving their value, people will realize they were never that valuable to begin with.

And so they keep running. Not because they love the chase, but because they don't know how to exist without it. Because if they're not striving, pushing, doing—then who are they?

They've tied their identity to their work, their worth to their output, their sense of security to their ability to keep going. They've built empires on effort, but not on the codes that make success sustainable.

And fear-built success? Never feels like success at all.

Because no matter how high you climb, how much money you make, how much validation you receive—it's never enough to make you feel safe.

There's always the next thing. The next milestone. The next reason to prove yourself again.

And that's why, no matter how much you grow, you don't feel free.

Because you never actually let yourself arrive.

The Lie That Success Will Save You

The world glorifies the hustle. The chase.

The idea that if you just push a little harder, do a little more, you'll finally hit that point where it all clicks.

Where the doubt disappears. Where you finally feel like you've made it.

But here's what they don't tell you:

That point doesn't exist.

It's an illusion. A mirage on the horizon that keeps shifting every time you think you're getting close.

You tell yourself:

Once I hit six figures, then I'll feel secure.

Once I have a waitlist of clients, then I'll trust myself.

Once I get recognized in my industry, then I'll stop doubting whether I belong here.

But you get there—and nothing changes.

Because the real issue was never the number in your bank account, the size of your audience, or the validation from others.

The real issue is whether you believe you're safe to succeed at all.

If deep down, you're still afraid of losing it...

If deep down, you don't trust yourself to sustain it...

If deep down, you still feel like you have something to prove...

Then no amount of external proof will ever be enough.

Success doesn't fix a broken identity.

It doesn't erase the doubts that have been running your mind for years.

It doesn't magically make you feel worthy, confident, or safe.

Because success isn't just about what you achieve. It's about whether your identity can hold it.

And if your mind is still wired for survival—if your nervous system still associates success with stress, pressure, and never-enoughness—then you'll continue to sabotage, struggle, and shrink the second you start to rise.

Not because you aren't capable.

Not because you don't want it.

But because part of you still believes success isn't safe.

What You're Really Here to Remember

The way out isn't about doing more—it's about becoming someone new.

There is a different way to lead.

A deeper kind of power.

One that doesn't come from strategy or proving, but from identity, embodiment, and emotional mastery.

Inside these pages, I'll walk you through the exact process I've used with high-level clients and entrepreneurs to help them interrupt the old identity patterns keeping them stuck—so they can expand into who they're here to become.

You'll learn how to:

- Understand and rewire your triggers in real-time using the Trigger Response Method™ (TRM)

- Release the hidden beliefs that cause you to shrink, perform, or overcompensate

- Move from reactive survival patterns into embodied leadership

- Lead yourself and others without needing to prove, push, or earn your worth

And partway through this book, you'll be introduced to The Expansion Code™—a set of seven identity-altering truths designed to help you break through hidden ceilings and fully embody the next level of your leadership, success, and personal freedom.

These aren't just concepts to remember.

They're codes to live by.

The kind you come back to when fear gets loud, when doubt resurfaces, or when an old pattern tries to pull you back.

They are the anchor points that remind you: *You've already outgrown who you used to be.* Now it's time to lead like it.

This isn't a book about fixing yourself.

It's a book about coming home to the version of you who never needed fixing to begin with.

So if you've ever felt like no amount of success could quiet the doubt...

If you've found yourself shrinking at the exact moment you were meant to expand...

If you're done performing, proving, or carrying pressure just to feel worthy of what you've already earned...

You're in the right place.

Let's break the pattern.

Let's rewrite the story.

Let's expand.

Chapter One

The Ceiling You Didn't Know You Built

You've done everything right. You've built something real—something that's growing, expanding, proving itself. The numbers are climbing. The opportunities are flowing. People are paying attention.

But here's what you might not realize yet: you're already embodying pieces of the Expansion Code™—even if you haven't named it. The subtle shifts are happening. You're showing up with more awareness, more pause, more presence. You're not stuck at the beginning—you're standing at the edge of what comes next. And with that edge comes hesitation.

It starts as a whisper, a fleeting thought you brush off at first.

What if this doesn't last?

What if this isn't as solid as I think it is?

What if I'm not actually as good as they think I am?

But the whisper doesn't fade—it lingers. It grows louder.

Now, instead of hitting send, you're rereading the email for the fifth time, searching for mistakes that aren't there. Instead of launching, you're tweaking and refining, convinced that it needs just *one more* adjustment. Instead of celebrating how far you've come, you're already bracing for what could go wrong.

You tell yourself it's just caution, just being strategic. But deep down, something else is at play.

You start second-guessing the offer you were excited about just last week. You convince yourself you need more time, more clarity, more certainty.

So you hold back.

Not outright. Not in a way that anyone would notice. You're too good at what you do for that.

Instead, you do the high-achiever version of self-sabotage:

- You tweak things endlessly instead of launching them.

- You tell yourself you're "just being strategic" while avoiding the move that actually stretches you.

- You take on more work to justify the success you already have—so you never have to sit with the discomfort of just *receiving* it.

- You downplay your wins. You shrink just a little. You hesitate before stepping fully into what you know is yours.

And the most frustrating part?

You don't even see it happening.

It feels logical—like you're just being careful, just making sure everything is aligned. But in reality, it's hesitation disguised as strategy.

You convince yourself you're just waiting for the right moment, the right sign, the right level of certainty. But how many times have you done that before? How many times have you convinced yourself you need just a little more preparation before you move?

The hesitation isn't logical. It's deeply wired, an unseen force pulling you back the moment things start to get too good, too easy, too expansive. And if you don't recognize it for what it is, you'll stay stuck in this pattern—always feeling on the verge of something bigger but never quite stepping into it.

What Is the Invisible Ceiling, Really?

Sarah was one of the most driven entrepreneurs I had ever coached. She had built her business from the ground up, pouring in countless hours, showing up relentlessly, and pushing herself beyond what most people would dare. When she finally crossed the six-figure mark, I expected her to feel relief, excitement—maybe even a sense of ease.

Instead, she panicked.

Almost overnight, she started pulling back. She hesitated before taking on new opportunities, overcomplicated simple decisions, and began doubting things she had once been confident about. She told herself she needed more clarity before her next big move. That she had to make sure everything was perfect before launching her next offer. That she wasn't *quite* ready.

Sound familiar?

At first, she didn't see what was happening. She thought she was just being cautious, making strategic choices. But as we peeled back the layers, we uncovered the truth: she had unknowingly hit her invisible ceiling.

The invisible ceiling isn't about external limits—it's about the internal limits you didn't know you'd accepted.

It's not about doing more, learning more, or proving more. It's about what you believe you're allowed to hold.

It's about —what you believe you're allowed to have.

And the wildest part?

You probably don't even realize it's there.

This ceiling was shaped long before you ever set foot in business, leadership, or personal development. It wasn't something you consciously chose—it was something that happened to you, reinforced in subtle ways over years, until it became the framework through which you see yourself and the world.

It's why some people stay stuck in the same income range year after year, never quite able to break through, even when they know they should be making more. It's why some entrepreneurs slow down the moment they start gaining momentum, unconsciously pulling back just before they hit their next level. It's why you can feel like you're too much and not enough at the same time—constantly navigating the tension between wanting more and fearing what might happen if you actually get it.

This limit wasn't built by logic. It was shaped by the stories you absorbed—about success, about struggle, about what's allowed for you.

Maybe you grew up in a household where success was always attached to struggle, so when things start flowing easily, you sabotage it because it doesn't feel earned. Maybe you were the overachiever who was always praised for working harder than everyone else, so when success starts coming effortlessly, you feel guilty. Maybe you were taught not to be "too much," so when you step into more visibility, you suddenly feel exposed and want to shrink. Maybe you watched people in your family work themselves to the bone without catching a break, so now, even though you've broken through, part of you still feels like *you have to struggle*—because ease feels unnatural, unearned, and unsafe.

These beliefs don't just sit in your mind. They live in your patterns, in the way you approach decisions, in the way you subconsciously hold yourself back. Every time you get close to stepping fully into what's next, you find yourself pausing—convincing yourself that it's not the right time, that you need more preparation, that you're not quite there yet.

Expansion Only Feels Scary When It's New

So what if I told you the fear isn't the flaw—it's the flag.

A sign that your internal ceiling is being challenged. That your nervous system is brushing up against the exact edge it was taught to avoid. This is where the Expansion Code™ quietly begins to activate—long before you ever name it. Not in big declarations, but in micro-decisions. In the moment you pause and choose to stay present instead of pull back.

You don't need to work harder. You don't need to prove yourself more. You need to learn to trust yourself with more—without shrinking, sabotaging, or pulling back.

If your patterns have kept you playing at the same level, then no amount of strategy will change your reality. You can build the most successful business, have the best opportunities, and still find yourself stuck in the same patterns. Because success isn't just about what you *do*—it's about what you believe you're *allowed* to have.

The real work isn't in doing more—it's in expanding your capacity to hold more.

Sarah was starting to see it. As we worked together, I asked her to consider a radical idea:

What if nothing was actually wrong?

What if she wasn't failing to keep up with her next level but rather adjusting to the idea that ease and success could exist together?

At first, she resisted the thought. She told me she had always been someone who thrived under pressure, who needed urgency to perform at her best. But urgency wasn't what was driving her anymore—it was fear. The fear of stepping fully into success without the safety net of struggle.

So I asked her, *What would happen if you allowed yourself to believe that it could be easy?* If she didn't need to hustle to prove herself? If she trusted that she was already worthy of the next level without having to fight for it?

And that's when it clicked.

The discomfort she was feeling wasn't a warning sign—it was growth. She wasn't backsliding or losing momentum; she was simply learning to exist in a new space where success wasn't built on overworking, over-proving, or overcomplicating.

What if the fear wasn't a stop sign, but a doorway?

A signal that you're standing at the edge of expansion? What if hesitation wasn't a signal that you're not ready but proof that you're on the edge of something new?

Expansion isn't about forcing your way through re-sistance. It's about recognizing when the fear you feel is simply your mind adjusting to a new level of possibility.

So let me ask you:

- *What if success didn't have to come with struggle?*

- *What if the feeling of discomfort was actually growth—your mind learning that more is safe?*

- *What would you do today if you already knew you were capable of holding more?*

The moment Sarah made that shift, everything changed. She stopped waiting for clarity and started trusting her instincts again. She took bold action—not because she was sure of every detail but because she finally understood that she didn't need certainty to move forward.

Once you learn to move beyond your invisible ceiling, success isn't something you chase—it's something you live in. And once you expand beyond your current limits—there is no going back.

What if the thing holding you back is actually the key to your next level?

You don't need to work harder. You don't need to prove yourself more. You need to learn to trust yourself with more—without shrinking, sabotaging, or pulling back.

If your patterns have kept you playing at the same level, then no amount of strategy will change your reality. You can build the most successful business, have the best opportunities, and still find yourself stuck in the same patterns.

It's not about what you're building—it's about what you subconsciously keep pushing away.

Rewrite the Story That Built Your Ceiling

It's one thing to notice where you stop short. It's another to rise anyway. Awareness alone won't break the cycle. You have to actively rewrite your limits by making new choices, taking different actions, and stepping into the version of yourself who already lives beyond that ceiling.

Sarah's biggest breakthrough didn't come from doing more. It came when she stopped waiting for permission. She stopped searching for certainty and started trusting herself to handle whatever came next. The moment she realized she didn't need struggle to prove she was worthy of success, everything changed. Her business grew—not because she suddenly had a better strategy but because she finally allowed herself to expand without holding back.

The same is true for you.

So ask yourself:

- *Where have I been holding back—not because I'm unready, but because I'm afraid of what comes next?*

- *What if success didn't have to come with struggle?*

- *What would I do today if I already knew I was capable of holding more?*

You don't have to wait for proof. You don't have to wait for permission. You don't have to wait until you feel completely ready.

You just have to decide that you're done shrinking.

You're Not Waiting—You're Expanding

Find one moment today where your nervous system wants to shrink—and choose to stretch instead. Speak the idea. Raise the price. Press publish. The move doesn't need to be perfect. It just needs to be different than the one fear would have made for you. That's how you rewire your response. That's how you signal to your system: *we're safe to rise now.*

You're not here to prove anything. You're here to practice who you're becoming. And every time you choose that version of you—the one who acts from truth, not fear—you build the muscle of expansion.

This isn't about waiting for confidence. It's about building capacity.

And that capacity? It only grows through action.

So the real question becomes: will you let the fear define your next step, or will you choose something new—even when it stretches you?

Because the moment you stop waiting and start moving differently, you crack the ceiling that's been holding you.

Chapter Two

The Trigger Is the Teacher

*Y*ou've spent your life chasing a version of power you thought you had to earn. Now, let's look at the silent forces that have been shaping who you think you are—and what it's actually costing you.

Why You Keep Reacting (Even When You Know Better)

I remember sitting on a Zoom call when a client questioned my strategy. My stomach dropped, my face flushed, and before I could catch it, that old familiar wave of self-doubt crashed in. It wasn't just their words—it was every memory of not feeling good enough or smart enough rushing to the surface. I didn't respond to their question—I responded to a thousand tiny echoes from my past, all layered beneath that one moment.

For a long time, I believed that if I did enough inner work, I'd eventually reach this place of complete emotional immunity. If I meditated enough, journaled enough, healed enough—I thought I'd become untouchable. The kind of person who was so grounded, so evolved, that nothing could shake me. I imagined floating through life in a kind of enlightened ease, where nothing set me off and everything rolled off my back.

That illusion didn't last.

Because the truth is—I still get triggered. You still get triggered. Every single person does. Triggers aren't a sign that something's gone wrong. They're a part of being human. But what I've learned after years of doing this work is this: while your triggers might never fully disappear, your relationship to them can completely transform.

This work doesn't mean you'll never be activated again. It means that when those emotions do rise, they don't pull you under. They don't derail your day. They don't spiral you into self-doubt, overanalyzing, or making everything mean something about your worth.

You begin to notice them.
Observe them.
And eventually, choose how to respond to them—with clarity, without collapse.

That's the real difference. Not in becoming someone who's never reactive—but in becoming someone who knows exactly how to move through it.

I used to react to everything. A comment, a look, a delay in response—I'd make up stories, assume the worst, and hand over my emotional stability to outside circumstances. I lived in a constant state of bracing. Bracing for judgment. Bracing for rejection. Bracing for the confirmation that maybe I wasn't actually good enough.

Until I realized: I didn't have to live like that. I didn't have to assign meaning to everything. I didn't have to carry the projections of others. I didn't have to spiral into stories that weren't mine to begin with.

And when I stopped doing that? Everything softened.

It wasn't that triggers stopped happening—it was that I stopped letting them take me out.

Now, when something rises up and activates an old wound, I know what to do.

I pause. I breathe. I observe. I ask myself, *What is this showing me?*

Not from a place of judgment or panic, but from curiosity. Because every trigger is a teacher. It holds information. Insight. A reflection of something that's still alive in your system. And when you meet it with awareness instead of avoidance, it loses its grip.

This is what emotional mastery really looks like—not bypassing your emotions, but learning how to lead yourself through them.

These moments might seem small, but they're powerful. They're the micro-moments that recalibrate how you move through the world. You might not realize it yet, but this is the beginning of a new foundation being laid.

One that doesn't rely on suppressing discomfort, but on expanding your capacity to hold it. One that doesn't chase perfection, but cultivates presence. One that, quietly and gradually, begins to reshape how you lead yourself—and everything else.

That's what makes you unshakable.

What Your Triggers Are Really Trying to Tell You

Triggers aren't random. They're patterned responses—deeply wired signals rooted in unresolved moments from your past, surfacing exactly when you least expect them.

Think about the last time something set you off.

Maybe it was something seemingly small. A client canceling last minute. A post not getting the engagement you expected. A friend's offhand comment that shouldn't have bothered you—but did.

On the surface, these things don't seem like a big deal. They're just normal parts of life, right?

And yet, your body reacted.

A tightness formed in your chest. A rush of frustration or self-doubt washed over you. Your heart rate sped up. Maybe you even felt the urge to lash out, shut down, or spiral into overthinking.

And suddenly, it wasn't just about the thing that happened—it was about what it *meant*.

It wasn't just a canceled client. It was proof that you weren't valuable.

It wasn't just a post that flopped. It was confirmation that your voice doesn't matter.

It wasn't just an offhand comment. It was a reminder of every moment you've ever felt misunderstood, unseen, or rejected.

This is what a trigger does. It takes a present moment and links it to a past wound. It magnifies the situation. It makes a five-second interaction feel like a personal attack. It turns a neutral event into an emotional reaction that feels far bigger than the moment itself.

Because the reaction isn't about what's happening now.

It's about everything similar you've ever experienced before.

Every time you felt dismissed. Every time you felt not good enough. Every time you felt unseen, undervalued, or unworthy.

Why Your Body Reacts Before You Can Think

To fully understand your triggers, you need to understand how your brain processes threats—because that's exactly how your nervous system perceives them.

Your brain's number one job isn't to make you happy. It's not focused on helping you grow or guiding you toward success. Its primary function is survival—keeping you safe according to what it's learned "safe" looks like.

And here's where it gets tricky: your brain doesn't evaluate safety based on what's logical or expansive. It evaluates safety based on what's familiar. So even if something is good for you—more money, more visibility, more intimacy—if it feels unfamiliar, your system may interpret it as unsafe.

That's why a perfectly harmless situation—a quiet client, a vague comment, a bold decision—can suddenly send your nervous system into overdrive. Your body reacts not to the facts of the moment, but to what that moment reminds it of. Even if the circumstances are completely different. Even if the rational part of your mind knows better.

Because your body doesn't speak logic. It speaks memory.

When the Past Takes Over the Present

Let's break it down.

You receive criticism from a client.

Your logical brain should be able to say, *Oh, this is just one person's opinion.*

But instead, your nervous system does something different—it starts searching for a past experience that felt similar.

If you were judged, rejected, or criticized in a way that hurt before—and if that moment left an emotional wound—your brain flags this as the same type of threat.

Now, suddenly, you're not just reacting to this moment.

You're reacting with the full emotional weight of every similar experience you've ever had.

And that's why your reaction feels so big—because it's not just about this one moment.

It's about everything that came before it.

It's about every version of you that was made to feel:

Small.

Inadequate.

Unworthy.

Rejected.

Not enough.

And because your nervous system is wired for survival, it doesn't take chances.

It doesn't pause to ask, *Is this really a threat?*

It doesn't analyze, *Is this situation different than before?*

It doesn't check to see, *Am I more capable of handling this now?*

It reacts.

Instantly.

Because in the primitive part of your brain, hesitation = danger.

The Hidden Cost of Staying in Reaction

Now you already know—your brain doesn't see the world through a neutral lens. It filters everything through your past experiences, especially the painful ones.

Every time you went through something emotionally intense—a rejection, a failure, a deep embarrassment, a moment of abandonment—your nervous system didn't just log the memory. It recorded the emotional charge

that came with it. The fear. The shame. The disappointment. The panic.

Even years later, even after all the healing, growth,
and expansion you've done—your brain can still register
moments like these as the same kind of threat.

If you grew up being judged for mistakes, even light
feedback can feel like an attack.

If you've faced abandonment, even subtle disconnection
in a relationship can feel like loss.

If success was always conditional on proving your worth,
moments of ease may feel unsafe—like you haven't
earned the right to receive without the struggle.

It's not logical. It's deeply wired emotional condition-
ing.

That's why triggers don't just feel uncomfortable—they feel overwhelming. You've probably had
moments where your reaction felt way bigger than the
situation called for. One minute you're steady, and the
next, it's like a surge of emotion hijacks your entire system.

Maybe it's instant rage over something small.

Sudden anxiety in a moment where you'd normally feel
confident.

Or a wave of shame that hits like it just happened—even when it doesn't make sense.

When your system registers discomfort, it moves straight into survival mode. Without realizing it, you slip into your most familiar coping pattern—whether that's shutting down, lashing out, people-pleasing, or freezing altogether.

You might find yourself snapping at someone before you even understand why.

Withdrawing suddenly and emotionally checking out.

Over-explaining or apologizing just to smooth things over.

Or feeling completely frozen—like you can't act at all.

Your body responds as if you're in real danger—even when it's just an emotional trigger.

Because your nervous system is still pulling from old emotional files, you repeat the same response patterns. You snap at a partner—not because of what they just said, but because it echoed an old wound. You spiral into doubt over a business decision—because it mirrors a past failure. You procrastinate on a big opportunity—because uncertainty still feels like danger.

Unless you learn how to interrupt this cycle, it will keep repeating. Not because the moment truly calls for it. Not because you're too sensitive. But because your system is still running an outdated survival script.

One that's long overdue for an upgrade.

Interrupting the Pattern

So if this is all happening automatically, how do you change it?

You train your nervous system to handle triggers differently.

Because right now, your brain only knows how to do one thing when it detects a threat:

React.

But what if, instead of reacting, you could pause?

What if, instead of spiraling, you could regulate?

What if, instead of falling into old patterns, you could choose a new response?

That's exactly what happens when you start doing the work of emotional mastery.

You stop living at the mercy of your reactions.

You start seeing them for what they are: a learned response—not the truth of who you are.

You start creating space between the trigger and your response.

And that space?

That's where all your power is.

But first, you have to recognize the signs that you're in reaction mode—because awareness is what allows you to shift.

Here's how you know you've been triggered:

- You feel a sudden tightening in your chest, throat, or stomach.

- You have the urge to blame someone else, even if you know it's not fully their fault.

- You feel the need to "fix" the situation immediately—even if nothing needs fixing.

- You start overthinking, people-pleasing, or trying to control what's happening.

- You feel pulled to shut down, lash out, or retreat.

These are your signals.

They're not signs that something's wrong with you. They're signs that something old is being activated—and that you're about to fall into a default pattern if you don't intervene.

Let me show you what this looks like in real life.

One of my clients, Lisa, used to spiral every time a client canceled on her. Logically, she knew cancellations were normal, but emotionally, it sent her into a tailspin of self-doubt. Her brain immediately pulled up old stories— *"I'm not good enough"* and *"I'm doing something wrong."*

After working together, Lisa committed to practicing the pause. The next time a cancellation happened, she felt the familiar wave of panic rise, but instead of reacting, she paused. She noticed the tightness in her chest and the urge to overcorrect—but she stayed with the discomfort, took a breath, and grounded herself.

From that space, she chose a calm, clear response. She sent a professional reply to the client, then moved on without spiraling. The story didn't own her anymore—because she had created space to choose something different.

That's where you get to rewrite the story.

Because the moment you realize *Oh, this isn't actually about what's happening right now. This is my nervous system reacting to something from the past*—you're no longer controlled by it.

You can step outside the reaction.

You can observe it without attaching meaning to it.

You can respond with clarity instead of reacting from fear.

And the more you practice this?

The less power your triggers have over you.

Not because they disappear.

Not because you force yourself to stop feeling them.

But because they stop feeling like threats.

And when something isn't a threat, your nervous system doesn't overreact.

That's what true healing looks like.

Not never getting triggered.

But knowing exactly what to do when it happens—so it doesn't own you anymore.

From Emotional Whiplash to Grounded Self-Leadership

When you begin to see your triggers for what they are—signals, not threats—you stop living at the mercy of your emotions and start leading your experience with intention.

Discomfort doesn't disappear. You won't float through life untouched by challenge. But when it rises, you don't collapse. You stay conscious. You breathe. You meet it with grounded awareness, not urgency. You recognize the story without becoming it. You witness the emotion without letting it hijack your response.

And in that space—between what's rising and how you choose to respond—is where your power lives.

This isn't just a mindset shift. It's a quiet recalibration of identity. Each moment of awareness becomes a vote for the future you're building.

And every time you pause, notice, and respond with presence, you reinforce a new pattern. You teach your nervous system that safety exists in the unfamiliar. You rewire your subconscious to expect ease instead of chaos. And most importantly—you prove, moment by moment, that you don't have to live in reaction.

You get to lead—on purpose.

The New Loop

They're your shortcut to growth, clarity, and emotional mastery—if you're willing to face them head-on. These are the moments where deeper frameworks begin to take root—the kind you'll soon learn to recognize more clearly.

Because every time a trigger arises, it's an opportunity to:

1. See what's really driving your reactions (the old pattern).

2. Choose something different (the new response).

3. Expand your capacity to hold success, ease, and emotional freedom.

The more you do this, the faster you'll evolve.

And this isn't about bypassing or spiritually shaming yourself into being "above" discomfort. This is about becoming someone who isn't owned by discomfort anymore.

Someone who can feel it fully—without letting it hijack their life.

Building the Muscle of Awareness

We're not going to complicate this. This isn't about "fix-ing" yourself or rushing into a whole new method—yet.

Right now, the most powerful thing you can do is to build the capacity to observe.

Because awareness alone shifts more than people real-ize.

1. Learn to Pause Before the Pattern Pulls You

Start noticing the exact moment you feel that emotional jolt—the tightening in your chest, the wave of frustra-tion, the sudden urge to shut down or lash out.

The goal isn't to fix it or even to change it yet.

Just pause.

Feel the reaction without feeding it.

Breathe.

This alone—pausing long enough to notice instead of react—is one of the most transformative skills you will ever build.

2. Ask, "What's This Really Showing Me?"

The next time you feel triggered, resist the urge to spiral or suppress.

Instead, get curious.

Ask yourself:

What is this showing me about how I've been operating beneath the surface?

No fixing. No judging. No overanalyzing.

Just *seeing*.

Because right now, the most important shift you can make is simply to stop defaulting to the old cycle of "reaction, story, spiral."

Just pause and observe—without needing to control or change it yet.

That's how you create space.

That's how you begin to build real emotional freedom.

Where Ownership Becomes Identity

Here's what rarely gets acknowledged:

The version of you who is waiting for triggers to disappear before you feel safe, powerful, or worthy will be waiting forever.

But the version of you who can stand in the storm, feel the wind hit your face, and stay grounded anyway?

That's the version that becomes unstoppable.

The one who knows discomfort may visit—but doesn't have to move in.

The one who understands that feeling triggered isn't failure—it's feedback.

The one who recognizes that every uncomfortable emotion is simply pointing you back to your next level of growth.

Because when you stop being afraid of your triggers, when you stop shrinking from them, you don't just change how you feel.

You change how you move.

How you lead.

How you live.

You become someone who no longer reacts to life—but creates it.

You're not just managing your emotions—you're rewiring your reality. This is where deep self-leadership begins. Where your default reactions stop running the show—and a new internal framework starts to emerge.

Because emotional freedom isn't about waiting for a life without challenges. It's about becoming the person who can meet every challenge from a grounded, powerful place—without collapsing into old patterns.

You were never meant to live in reaction mode.You were meant to lead, create, and expand from a place of deep self-trust.

When you stop fighting your triggers and start listening to them, you stop repeating the old story of survival—and step into the new story of expansion.

Because every time you pause, every time you choose to respond with clarity instead of fear, every time you stay present instead of shrinking back—you are building the capacity to hold more.

More ease.

More success.

More emotional freedom.

That is the foundation for everything you're here to create.

That is how you become unshakable—not because life gets easier, but because you do.

Because when you master yourself, you master the game.

That's when it clicks: *it was never about dodging the storm. It was about becoming the calm within it—and realizing the storm was never bigger than you.*

The moment you stop shrinking from discomfort is the moment you begin expanding into who you were always meant to be.

Keep going.

There's more waiting for you—more freedom, more truth, more of yourself than you've ever let fully come to the surface.

You don't know it yet—but you're already laying the foundation for a new way of leading yourself. The kind that doesn't just change how you respond—but who you become.

Once you realize your identity is running the show, the next question becomes: why do we keep repeating patterns that don't serve us? The answer lives in the hidden pay-off—the part of you that's been benefiting from staying exactly where you are.

Chapter Three

The Hidden Payoff: Why Playing Small Still Feels Safe

B efore we talk about rewiring anything, we have to get honest about why the old patterns are still gripping you.

I used to think self-sabotage was irrational. Why would I actively block my own success? Why would I procrastinate on things that mattered? Why would I hold myself back from opportunities I knew could change everything?

It didn't make sense—until I realized something that changed everything for me.

I wasn't sabotaging myself because I wanted to fail. I was sabotaging myself because, on some level, staying stuck felt safer than moving forward.

That's the hard truth most people don't talk about. You don't hold onto limiting beliefs and behaviors for no reason. There is always a hidden payoff—a subconscious benefit you're getting from staying exactly where you are.

What's Really Keeping You Stuck

Maybe this sounds familiar:

You've got a notebook full of ideas, half-written sales pages, and programs you've been "almost ready" to launch for months. Each time you get close, you tell yourself, *"I just need to tweak this one more thing,"* or *"It's not the right time yet."* The truth is, you've been circling the runway but never taking off.

Or maybe you're already out there—delivering incredible value, coaching your heart out—but still charging less than you know you should. You're overdelivering in every session, every offer, every post, while secretly wondering why it still feels like you're coming up short.

And then there's the momentum: The momentum builds—then suddenly, you pull back the moment visibility or success feels too close.

You ghost your email list. You stop posting. You start doubting your work, convincing yourself you need to "regroup" before you move forward.

Sound familiar?

On the surface, these patterns look like common issues: fear, perfectionism, imposter syndrome, procrastination. But underneath, there's always something deeper keeping you locked in place.

Because the hidden payoff is quietly pulling the strings.

If you don't launch, you don't have to risk failure. If you don't raise your rates, you don't have to risk rejection. If you don't get too big, too successful, or too visible, you don't have to deal with the pressure of sustaining it.

You might think you're 'playing it safe.' But what you're really doing is protecting the version of you who isn't sure they're ready to rise yet.

Not the actual success—but the emotional weight your subconscious has attached to it: the fear of judgment, the fear of loss, the fear of the unknown.

So while you consciously crave expansion, the deeper, protective part of you is quietly whispering:

"Stay here. This is familiar. This is safe."

The Pattern That Made Me Feel Powerful (Until It Didn't)

For years, I thrived on chaos.

I used to wear it like a badge of honor. The late nights, the impossible deadlines, the last-minute saves—they became the fabric of my identity. I prided myself on being the one who could handle what others couldn't. The one who came alive when everything felt like it was falling apart.

I told myself I worked best under pressure, that I needed the adrenaline of high stakes to do my best work. And for a while, it felt true. It felt powerful.

But underneath that power? There was fear.

The hidden payoff? I got to feel like an overcomer. Like I was invincible in the face of chaos.

What I didn't realize was that I was unconsciously curating my environment to match that identity.

I wasn't sabotaging myself because I wanted to fail—I was unconsciously creating fires so I could feel powerful when I put them out.

Here's how it played out: juggling too many projects at once, waiting until the very last second to make critical decisions, ignoring red flags until they became fires.

The problem? That "resilience" became my cage.

It kept me stuck in cycles of overwhelm, overextension, and unnecessary stress.

And it wasn't just in my business.

I found myself repeating this in relationships, in my health, and even in my personal growth journey.

If it wasn't hard, it didn't feel like I was doing it "right."

I avoided ease because ease didn't feel earned.

I overcomplicated launches because if it felt too simple, I couldn't trust it.

I micromanaged success because the idea of ease felt like a risk.

And maybe you're reading this and realizing you've done something similar.

Maybe you've mistaken survival for mastery. Maybe you've confused constant tension with real growth.

What I've learned is this: just because you can thrive under pressure doesn't mean you have to keep proving it.

Sometimes the bravest thing you can do is allow things to be easy—and trust that ease doesn't make you less capable, it makes you more available for the life you actually want.

The Payoffs That Quietly Sabotage High-Achievers

When you start unpacking your patterns, you might expect to find fear, doubt, maybe even perfectionism. But what you don't always expect to find is comfort.

That's the tricky part about self-sabotage—it doesn't just hold you back. It protects you. It gives you a sense of control. It helps you feel safe... even when it's also keeping you stuck.

Some payoffs are loud and obvious. Others hide in your logic. They sound like smart decisions. They dress themselves up as strategy. But beneath the surface, they're quietly shaping what you believe you're allowed to have.

Let's name them—because the moment you see your pattern, you stop being run by it.

The Payoff of Protection

"If I don't fully go for it, I can't fully fail."

You tell yourself you're waiting for clarity. That it's just not the right time yet. That you need to refine the offer, get more testimonials, clean up your backend systems first.

But the truth? Staying in the prep phase is safer than launching into the unknown. As long as you're preparing, you're protected from disappointment. From rejection. From the moment where the dream meets reality and someone might not say yes.

Even in your career, maybe you've stayed where it feels steady. You're competent. You're praised. But deep down, you know you've outgrown it. That next level keeps tugging at you—but going for it means risking the chance you won't rise the way you hope.

So you stay. And you tell yourself it's responsible. Smart. Strategic.

But what if it's just fear wearing a suit?

The Payoff of Familiarity

"If I stay in this pattern, I don't have to face the unknown."

Even when you're tired of the hustle... even when the cycle feels like a loop you can't break... it still feels oddly comfortable. Because at least you know how to survive here.

You know how to handle the hard. You've built a whole identity around being the one who can carry it all. The chaos, the deadlines, the push-pull—it's not ideal, but it's familiar. And familiarity registers as safety to your system.

So when something easier tries to come in—when there's space, flow, or softness—you flinch. You question it. You overcomplicate it. Because if it doesn't feel like a fight, can it really be trusted?

The truth is, the unknown might hold more peace, more success, more freedom... but it also holds unpredictability. And your nervous system might still think *predictable discomfort* is safer than unfamiliar ease.

The Payoff of Control

"If I don't get too big, I don't have to carry more."

This one sneaks in when things are actually going well.

You start gaining traction. People are watching. The momentum is building. And suddenly—you feel the weight of being seen. Of being expected to keep it all going. Of being the one others look to, rely on, believe in.

So what do you do? You scale back. You ghost your audience. You lower your visibility. You avoid the big move that would take you to your next level.

Why? Because rising feels like responsibility. And if you rise too high, you might not be able to come down without someone noticing. So staying just below your true potential gives you the illusion of control.

But the truth? Carrying a version of yourself that's half-expressed is just as heavy—if not heavier—than the pressure you're trying to avoid.

The Payoff of Being Relatable

"If I don't outgrow this level, I don't make people uncomfortable."

Let's be honest—growth can be lonely. Especially when the people around you are used to a version of you that's a little smaller, a little softer, a little more familiar.

So maybe you edit yourself in conversations. Diminish your wins. Quiet your ambition around people who don't quite "get it." You shrink not because you're not ready—but because you're afraid your evolution might shift the dynamic.

This isn't just about business—it's identity. Maybe the people you love knew you before the growth. Before you found your voice. Before you started becoming this version of you.

And a part of you doesn't want to leave anyone behind. So you keep yourself at a level that keeps everyone comfortable... even if it costs you your expansion.

But here's what might surprise you: The people you're afraid of outgrowing?

Some of them are waiting to see what's possible through you.

The Payoff of Avoiding Judgment

"If I never fully own it, I don't have to risk being criticized."

Visibility comes with opinions. Leadership comes with projections. Power comes with misunderstanding.

So it makes sense that you might hold back—not because you don't have something powerful to say, but because you're afraid of how it might land.

You write the post but don't hit publish. You pitch yourself—then ghost the follow-up. You soften your edges so no one gets uncomfortable.

Not because you're unsure of yourself—but because being seen in your full power feels vulnerable.

What if they don't like this version of you?

What if they talk?

What if they leave?

And yet—watering down your truth to avoid judgment will never give you the safety you're looking for.

Because the moment you stop dimming your light, yes—some people might fall away.

But the right ones?

They'll find you precisely *because* you turned it all the way on.

Your Personal Pattern Reveal

Now it's time to pull this in closer—right to where you are.

Let's strip away the theory for a second and make this personal.

Where's the place in your life where you feel like you've been circling the same loop? Maybe it's that big project you've been sitting on, telling yourself you're "almost ready." Maybe it's the promotion you keep considering but keep talking yourself out of. Or maybe it's the visibility you crave, but every time you start to show up, you disappear just as quickly.

Now, take a pause. Drop into the feeling of it.

Ask yourself this:

What do I actually gain from staying stuck here?

And I know—the knee-jerk reaction is probably, "Nothing! This sucks, and I want out." But let's get honest. What's hiding underneath the discomfort?

What's the thing you're secretly avoiding? Is it rejection? The possibility of failing publicly? The fear that success might change how people see you—or how you see yourself?

What am I shielding myself from by staying exactly where I am?

Maybe it's the anxiety that comes with new responsibility. Maybe it's the fear of setting bigger expectations and not living up to them. Or maybe it's the unknown—the part where you've never actually let yourself experience what happens when you do rise.

What feels "safe" about staying here, even if part of me is desperate for more?

This part rarely gets acknowledged

We don't stay stuck because we like it. We stay stuck because it feels safer than the alternative.

And finally, the question that usually unlocks the whole thing:

What do I believe will happen if I actually get what I say I want?

This is where you'll find the invisible grip.

This is where the invisible ceiling becomes visible—not as an external block, but as a part of your identity you've outgrown.

It's never just about fear of failure or fear of success. It's about what you've linked those things to—judgment, loss, abandonment, pressure.

At some point, you started tying your identity to staying here. Playing small became familiar—not just to your nervous system, but to your sense of self. The hesitation isn't just about survival anymore—it's about protecting the version of you who believes this is as far as you're allowed to go.

Because rising into more often means saying goodbye to old roles, old patterns, and old ways of seeing yourself—and that can feel just as risky as any external challenge.

But here's the power move:

Once you bring that pattern to the surface, you get your choice back.

You can keep running the old code—or you can decide to move differently.

And soon, you'll begin to see the deeper frameworks that make this shift possible—not as theory, but as embodied truth.

And that's what's coming next.

Because naming it is just the beginning.

The real shift happens when you choose to release it—and walk straight toward who you're becoming.

Because this work? This isn't about adding one more productivity hack or stacking more pressure on top of an already full plate.

This is about choosing yourself.

Choosing to live free of the unconscious scripts that have been running your life.

Choosing to become the version of you who no longer negotiates your power away for comfort or validation.

So as you sit with these questions, know this: Awareness is the crack where the light gets in. It's where your story starts to change.

And you don't have to rush it.

You don't have to "fix" yourself.

You just have to be willing to see your patterns clearly enough to decide, *"I'm not playing this out anymore."*

Because when you break free of the payoff—you don't just rise beyond the ceiling.

You rise into the version of you who's been waiting all along.

You unlock the version of yourself that fear was never strong enough to bury—only quiet.

The one who already knows how to hold it all—with ease, with certainty, and with power.

Knowing what holds you back is powerful. But knowing what to do in the moment you feel it rising? That's how you reclaim everything. It's time to master the five steps that change your response in real-time.

Chapter Four

Rewired in Real Time

efore you can fully embody the Codes, you have to know how to stay with yourself when it matters most. This is where we go first.

Still Human. Still Triggered. Still in Power.

True freedom was never about escaping your triggers.

It was about no longer mistaking them for truth.

By now, you've started to feel the difference. You've tasted what it's like to meet discomfort with presence instead of panic. You've paused in moments where you used to spiral. You've led yourself through reactions that once would've taken you out.

But I didn't always know how to do that.

For years, I believed freedom from my triggers meant eliminating them completely. That if I did enough healing, enough mindset work, enough journaling, I'd eventually reach a place where I was immune to the waves that used to knock me off course. I thought emotional mastery meant being untouched by discomfort—as if I'd become so evolved, nothing could shake me.

Now, here's what's actually real: I still get triggered sometimes. But I rarely get hooked in a way that lingers. I don't spiral for hours. I don't lose sleep replaying conversations or questioning my worth. I don't hand over my power to fleeting moments or old stories dressed in new clothing.

Does that mean life stopped throwing curveballs? Not even close. People still disappoint me. Unexpected challenges still show up. There are days when old narratives try to sneak back in and convince me to shrink. But the difference now is, I don't let those moments dictate how I show up. I don't let them hijack my clarity or authority.

That didn't happen overnight. I used to ride the same emotional rollercoaster most people are stuck on—soaring with the highs, crashing with the lows, feeling like my nervous system was always at the mercy of what was happening around me. My triggers felt like truth. My reactions felt automatic. My power felt out of reach.

And that's why this work matters so deeply. Because what I've learned—and what I want to show you here—is that you don't have to live on that ride forever. You don't have to be run by emotions you don't fully understand. You don't have to collapse every time life gets loud. You can actually train yourself to stay grounded, clear, and anchored—even in the heat of the moment.

This isn't about bypassing discomfort or pretending you're above emotional waves. It's not about "positive vibing" your way out of human experience. It's about reclaiming the ability to see what's really happening beneath the surface—and lead yourself through it with intention, not reaction.

That's what the Trigger Response Method (TRM) gives you: a map. Five powerful steps that interrupt the automatic loop of reactivity and hand your power back to the part of you that leads with clarity, presence, and emotional command.

This is where you stop defaulting to the old and begin integrating a new way of being—one rooted in self-trust, sovereignty, and true resilience.

You already know your triggers aren't random. You've seen how they mirror the past, how they echo old wounds, how they keep you repeating stories you never consciously chose.

Now it's time to do something about it.

The Loop You Didn't Know You Were In

Let's talk about the pattern most people don't even realize they're caught in—the invisible loop that plays out every time a trigger hits.

It starts innocently enough.

Someone says something offhanded. A client doesn't follow through. A post you were excited to share flops, or someone you admire questions your work.

And before you even realize it, your system is activated.

Maybe your stomach tightens. Maybe your chest feels heavy. Maybe you feel the urge to over-explain, defend, or shut down altogether.

What happens next? Without even pausing, you react.

Maybe you retreat and start second-guessing everything. Maybe you overcompensate—working harder, people-pleasing, bending over backwards. Or maybe you stay stuck in your head, replaying the situation over and over, building a case against yourself or the world.

What makes it so potent is that it's not just about what happened in the moment—it's about what that trigger taps into underneath.

Because the trigger doesn't just live in the now—it taps into every unresolved story from your past.

That client who ghosts you isn't just one client. It becomes proof that *"people can't be trusted,"* or *"I'm not cut out for this."* That critical comment on your post isn't just about your content—it reinforces the old belief that *"I'm not smart enough,"* or *"I'm always misunderstood."* That friend who cancels plans triggers something deeper like, *"I'm easy to abandon,"* or *"I'm not a priority."*

And once your brain links today's trigger to an old narrative, the story swallows you whole.

It's not just a reaction anymore—it's the lens you start seeing everything through.

You tell yourself: *"See, this always happens to me." "I knew I wasn't ready." "I knew this wasn't safe."*

And just like that, you're not responding to this moment—you're reacting from the residue of every moment that came before it.

The same loop, the same internal tug-of-war.

This is how most people live—chained to reactions they don't fully understand, stuck in cycles that feel personal but are really just unexamined patterns playing on repeat.

But what if it could be different?

What if you could interrupt that loop right in the middle of it?

What if, instead of collapsing into the story, you could step out of it—and choose a completely different response?

That's what TRM is here to help you do.

It's not about never being triggered again. It's about knowing exactly what to do when the trigger shows up, so you stop reacting like the version of you from the past—and start leading like the version of you that's building the future.

Step 1: Recognize the Trigger

Triggers don't show up with a warning sign. They happen fast—sometimes in a blink. One moment, you're cruising through your day, and the next, you're caught in a surge of emotion, wondering why you suddenly feel anxious, defensive, or frustrated.

By the time most people notice what's happening, they're already deep in reaction mode.

That's why the first step in TRM is simple but powerful: awareness.

It's about catching the very first spark—the split-second shift where you feel yourself get hooked.

This is the moment where your heart rate quickens when you feel heat rising in your chest, when your jaw clenches, when your mind starts racing ahead or spiraling back.

It's the "Oh, there it is" moment.

And here's the key: you're not here to analyze yet. You're not trying to "fix" anything. You're just becoming the observer.

Like noticing a storm cloud rolling in from the distance without scrambling to stop the rain.

You might feel the urge to react immediately—defend yourself, shut down emotionally, retreat, people-please, overthink. The pattern wants to pull you in fast, like a rip current.

But your job here is simply to *notice*.

Ask yourself:

- What just happened in the external world? What's the trigger itself—not my interpretation of it?

- Where do I feel this in my body? (Is there a tightness in my chest? A knot in my stomach? A heat behind my eyes?)

- What's the knee-jerk reaction rising up right now? (Do I want to lash out, prove something, disappear, or get busy fixing?)

And here's the deeper work: noticing without judging.

Most people layer shame onto their awareness: "I shouldn't be this bothered." "Why am I still getting triggered by this?" "Other people wouldn't react this way."

But judgment clouds the awareness you're building. Your goal is simply to observe without assigning meaning to the reaction yet.

Because when you can slow down just long enough to recognize what's happening as it happens, you open the doorway to change.

The trigger might be automatic. But your response? That's power you get to choose.

Step 2: Observe and Understand

Here's where most people lose themselves.

They recognize the trigger—maybe they even feel the heat of it—and then immediately either try to suppress it or let it take over.

You know the feeling:

- The inner dialogue that goes, "Why am I like this? I should be past this by now."

- Or the slide: "This always happens. I'll never break this cycle."

Neither one brings you any closer to freedom. Both responses pull you deeper into the emotional quicksand.

What we're doing here is different.

This is where you pause—not to stuff the emotion down, and not to feed it—but to *witness* it.

Imagine stepping outside of yourself for a moment. Like zooming out to see the whole emotional landscape without being swallowed by it.

Here's how you start:

- First, detach from the swirl. Instead of "I am triggered," shift to "I am noticing that I feel triggered." That small change separates you from the emotion and gives you breathing room.

- Next, label what you're feeling—not in a vague way like "I feel bad," but in a clear, specific way. Is it fear? Is it rejection? Is it shame? Is it frustration? The more precise you are, the more power you regain.

- Now, the hardest part for most people: replace self-judgment with compassionate curiosity.

Ask yourself:

- "What is this really about?"

- "What does this remind me of?"

- "Where have I felt this before?"

A trigger collapses time. What feels like a present reaction is often your past self stepping in to protect you—using the only tools it knew back then.

Maybe your friend cancelling dinner feels like abandonment—but it's really poking at a time you felt left out as a kid.

Maybe your client's feedback feels like criticism—but underneath, it's awakening the voice of a parent or teacher who made you feel like you could never do enough.

This step isn't about justifying anyone else's behavior or bypassing your own feelings.

It's about slowing down long enough to recognize:

- *This isn't just about now.*

- *This is about what's being reactivated beneath the surface.*

And the power in this? Once you see what's really being stirred up, you don't automatically hand your reaction over to it.

You start interrupting the pattern before it takes you on the ride.

Step 3: Identify the Payoff

Here's where the deeper work happens—the part where you shine a light on what's been quietly driving the bus all along.

Because by now, you've noticed the trigger. You've stepped out of autopilot. But there's still a reason why your system defaults to this pattern.

This is where we uncover *the payoff.*

Like it or not, there's always a payoff.

I know, most people hate hearing that. "Why would I be getting something from staying stuck?" It sounds counterintuitive—but that's exactly how the subconscious operates.

Even the patterns that frustrate you most, the ones that feel like they're holding you back, are serving some hidden purpose.

It might be protection.

It might be control.

It might be familiarity.

But there's always a reason you've kept this pattern alive.

So here's what we ask now:

- **What is this reaction protecting me from?** Are you avoiding rejection by playing small? Are you sidestepping discomfort by staying in confusion or delay? Are you keeping your nervous system safe by avoiding visibility?

- **How does staying in this pattern secretly serve me?** Does perfectionism give you an excuse not to risk criticism?Does procrastination protect you from fully owning your power—and what it might demand of you?Does staying in resentment reinforce an old belief that you're the underdog or the outsider, giving you a familiar identity to cling to?

- **What would actually happen if I let this go?** Would you feel exposed? Would you fear becoming unrelatable? Would you have to step into a level of leadership, abundance, or visibility that feels wildly uncomfortable—even if it's what you say you want?

What keeps most people stuck isn't logic—it's emotion.

It's rarely something you'd consciously *choose,* but subconsciously? It's been your safety blanket. It's been your self-protection strategy.

For example, if you're constantly triggered by criticism, the hidden payoff might be that staying small means no one can tear you down publicly. If you freeze every time someone overlooks you, the payoff could be that sitting in quiet resentment feels safer than risking vulnerability—and potentially being disappointed again. It's not always obvious, but it's there. And the moment you see it clearly, you take your power back.

And no, this isn't about blaming yourself. It's about *understanding* yourself.

Because once you name the emotional trade-off, you create the space to make a different choice.

You don't just rip the pattern away—you get to *decide* if it's still worth holding onto.

And when you realize that most of these payoffs are rooted in outdated fears or beliefs that no longer serve who you're becoming?

That's when things start to shift fast.

Step 4: The Choice Point

This is the moment where everything cracks open.

It's not just about making a different decision—it's about becoming someone new.

Because every time you pause at the Choice Point and choose power over pattern, you're not just responding differently.You're reintroducing yourself to the world as the version of you who leads, trusts, and rises.

The Choice Point isn't just where the trigger ends—it's where your next level begins.

The Choice Point is that tiny, powerful space between stimulus and response—the quiet pause where you wake up to the fact that you are no longer required to run the old pattern.

It's the fork in the road where you realize:

- You don't have to spiral into self-doubt.

- You don't have to over deliver to feel safe.

- You don't have to pull back when things get good.

You can choose to step into something new.

The Choice Point always exists. But the old pattern is so fast, so ingrained, that it sweeps people past the pause where change could have happened.

That's why this step is crucial.

You've caught the trigger.

You've observed it without judgment.

You've seen the hidden payoff.

Now, you stand in front of the door—and it's up to you whether you reach for the handle or stay where you've always been.

This is the moment to pause and ask yourself:

- If I were already the version of myself I'm becoming, how would I respond right now?

- What action would the most expanded, empowered version of me take in this situation?

- What response would create the result I actually want—instead of recreating the one I'm used to?

It sounds simple, but this is *the work*. The Choice Point is where you rewire everything.

Because every time you take a breath and consciously choose the aligned response—*instead* of defaulting to the one you've always chosen—you're literally shifting your neural pathways.

You're training your nervous system to believe that ease, leadership, expansion, and calm are safe to hold.

It's in these moments that you stop being at the mercy of your past.

You become the person who pauses before sending the reactive email.The person who shows up live even when self-doubt creeps in.The person who sets the boundary even though people-pleasing feels easier.

The beauty? The more you pause at the Choice Point, the more second nature it becomes.

It's like building a new muscle. In the beginning, it takes awareness and intention. Over time, it becomes your new baseline.

And that's the shift most people never make—not because they can't, but because they didn't know the space between trigger and reaction was there all along.

Your power lives inside that space.

Step 5: Choose Your Aligned Response

This is the moment where you reclaim your power—not in theory, but in practice.

Because awareness alone isn't enough. You can recognize the trigger, observe it, and even spot the hidden payoff, but until you *move differently*, the pattern stays alive.

This step is where you stop circling and finally shift.

Instead of reacting from autopilot—defaulting to over-giving, spiraling into overthinking, numbing out, or snapping back—you make a conscious decision to respond from your higher self, not your wound.

This could look like:

- Choosing to leave the text unread instead of jumping into a defensive explanation.

- Speaking your needs calmly in a conversation instead of people-pleasing to keep the peace.

- Saying yes to the opportunity that scares you, even though the old version of you would have played it safe.

- Walking away from the comparison trap online instead of letting it spiral into self-doubt.

The specifics don't matter as much as the energy behind them.

Because what you're really doing here is collapsing the old cycle—and proving to your nervous system that a new way is possible.

With each aligned response, you're sending a message to your brain: "We don't have to live inside this old story anymore."

This is neuroplasticity in action. The more you choose your higher self in real-time, the more you rewire your brain to default to empowered responses instead of reactive ones.

And here's what's even more powerful:

At first, these aligned responses will feel uncomfortable. They'll feel unfamiliar, maybe even awkward.

But eventually?

They become who you are.

They become how you naturally move through the world—with clarity, with leadership, with an unshakable calm that no longer gets hijacked by every trigger that crosses your path.

You stop being someone who "knows better" and start being someone who leads differently.

Someone who lives the work—not just understands it.

And that? That's how you break cycles—not just once, but every single day.

So how does this actually look when it matters most—in the moments you used to spiral, shut down, or freeze?

TRM in Motion: What It Looks Like in the Wild

One of the most common things I hear from my clients when they first begin working with me is, "I thought I was past this by now."

They're high-achievers. Smart, capable, driven. On paper, they've got it together. But under the surface? Triggers still override their clarity and shape decisions they later regret. Until we bring TRM into the picture.

Take Jenna, a client who came to me frustrated and exhausted. She was scaling her coaching business, but every time she gained momentum—new clients, bigger visibility—she'd unconsciously pull back.

The pattern? She'd get triggered the moment a client gave constructive feedback, even if it was kind and re-spectful. Suddenly, she'd spiral—questioning her abilities, feeling like an imposter, considering refunding clients just to "fix it."

When we applied TRM, everything shifted.

She caught the pattern early—recognizing that her nervous system was equating feedback with rejection. We walked through the payoff together: staying small protected her from risking criticism at a bigger level.

Once she named it, she hit her Choice Point. And instead of shrinking back, she leaned in. Jenna replied to her client with grounded clarity, took the feedback without personalizing it, and actually deepened the relationship as a result. Within months, she'd stopped ghosting during her launches and was showing up fully, without the emotional whiplash she'd been stuck in for years.

Then there's Marcus, a corporate leader who kept finding himself derailed by conflict. Anytime tension arose on his team, he'd default to micromanaging—believing it was his job to fix everything before it spiraled.

When we worked through TRM, he realized the hidden payoff: micromanaging gave him a false sense of control. It shielded him from the discomfort of trusting his team and risking things not going "perfectly."

At the Choice Point, Marcus chose something new. Instead of stepping in to "fix," he paused, got curious, and asked his team questions. The result? His leadership transformed. His team took more ownership, trust deepened, and Marcus found himself operating with far more ease—and less burnout.

And then there was Sarah, an entrepreneur who kept procrastinating on launching a new program, telling herself she needed "more time."

The trigger? Visibility. The payoff? Staying behind the scenes kept her safe from judgment.

Once she applied TRM, she realized her procrastination wasn't laziness—it was protection. At the Choice Point, she chose courage. She launched, imperfectly but powerfully, and signed clients within days.

The beauty of TRM isn't that it makes triggers disappear.

It's that it hands you the tools to navigate them—so that what used to derail you for days or weeks becomes a five-minute pause and a conscious decision.

The spiral shortens. The recovery time collapses. The leadership within you rises.

This is how you move from reacting on autopilot to responding with calm, clarity, and choice.

Because that's what true emotional mastery looks like.

Now it's your turn to step into this work—where theory becomes transformation.

Your Turn to Rewire

Before you move on, let's make this real for you.

Take a moment and think back to a situation—recent or past—where you know you got triggered.

What happened? Strip away the narrative and look at just the raw facts. What was the actual event?

Now, drop into your body for a second.

How did it feel in that exact moment? Not how you feel about it now—how did it feel when it hit? Was it a wave of heat? A tightening in your chest? A flush of anger or shame?

What story immediately came to the surface? Was it, *"I'm not good enough," "This always happens to me,"* or *"Why can't I get this right?"*

Here's where we dig deeper:

What might the hidden payoff have been? What were you protecting yourself from in that moment? What discomfort were you avoiding?

And now, with hindsight as your ally—if you could go back to that Choice Point, what aligned response would you choose instead?

Write it down. Let yourself feel it—not to fix it, but to reclaim it.

This isn't about getting it perfect. It's about building the muscle of noticing. Of choosing. Of breaking the loop when it matters most.

Because the more you practice TRM, the faster you reclaim your power—not just in one-off situations, but across every area of your life.

Every decision.

Every relationship.

Every opportunity to rise.

This is where your work shifts from theory to mastery.

Where you stop responding from old wounds and start moving from embodied leadership.

And when that shift happens?

You don't just feel different.

You become different.

And that's the version of you the world's been waiting for.

Chapter Five

The Choice Point — The Moment That Rewrites the Pattern

The power isn't just in recognizing your triggers—it's in what you choose next. There's a moment between reaction and response that can change everything. This is where power meets possibility.

The Most Important Second of Your Day

Here's how it actually plays out in real life. One of my clients—let's call her Tamara—used to freeze every time her team pushed back on one of her ideas. Even small, respectful feedback would send her spiraling into over-explaining, people-pleasing, and doubting her leadership. It wasn't until she learned to recognize the Choice Point that she realized her pattern wasn't about the team—it was about an old belief that being questioned meant being unsafe. By identifying that flicker of reactivity in real-time, Tamara began to breathe through those moments and respond as the confident leader she was becoming—not the little girl who once felt like her voice didn't matter.

There's a moment that lives right between the trigger and the spiral. A tiny, quiet opening that most people never notice—not because it isn't there, but because they've never been taught to look for it. It's that flicker of awareness where everything could change... if you let it.

This is what I call the Choice Point—the birthplace of a new kind of power.

Most people move through their day completely unaware of this opening—this brief interruption between stimulus and reaction that could change everything. They get triggered, they react, and they repeat. Not because they're incapable of change, but because their brains are conditioned to return to what's known—even when that familiarity quietly reinforces the very patterns they want to break.

So instead of interrupting the cycle, they defend. Instead of noticing, they numb. Instead of choosing something new, they repeat the pattern that feels safest. And then they wonder why, after all the inner work, they still end up in the same cycles.

If you've ever caught yourself mid-reaction thinking, *"Here I go again,"* you've brushed up against the Choice Point. That moment of recognition—of noticing the old reaction before it fully takes over—is the beginning of everything. It's the place where you get to disrupt the script you've been reading from for years.

But learning to use it? That's the real work.

This chapter is about building the muscle to not just recognize the Choice Point, but to stretch that gap wide enough that you can make a decision rooted in who you're becoming—not who you've always defaulted to.

Not from force. Not from perfection. But from the kind of grounded awareness that changes everything from the inside out.

This isn't mindset theory or fluffy self-help. This is about building a real, embodied skill set to lead yourself differently when it counts most.

Because that split-second pause? That's not just where your power lives.

That's where your future begins.

The Quiet Split Second That Can Change Everything

The Choice Point is where your history meets your possibility—and where you decide which one leads.

The Choice Point is that often-missed moment when something in you realizes: *I don't have to do what I've always done.* It's the space between being emotionally activated and doing what you've always done next—whether that's shutting down, over-explaining, retreating, lashing out, or slipping into a story that's not even true.

Most people blow right past this space because it happens fast. It's subtle. It doesn't scream for your attention—it whispers. And if you don't know how to listen for it, you'll miss it. Every time.

But when you do catch it? When you interrupt the rhythm—notice the rise of heat in your chest, the tightening in your gut, the story starting to spin in your mind—and you create even a sliver of awareness? That's the Choice Point. That's the moment where an entirely new path becomes available.

Let's say a client sends a message that feels passive-aggressive. Normally, your nervous system would fire off a flood of responses—anxiety, over-analysis, tension. But this time, you pause. You notice the rising heat, the shallow breath, the narrative trying to hook you. And in that pause, you ask: What's actually happening here? What version of me do I want to lead this moment?

The Choice Point isn't about becoming robotic or detached. It's about choosing presence in a world that trains you to react on autopilot. It's about reclaiming authorship of the moment right before your old story takes over. It's about catching yourself before you slip back into who you've always been. It's about choosing alignment over your old programming.

And the more you recognize this space, the more power you gain over how you show up—in your business, your relationships, and your own internal world.

Because, remember—triggers themselves are neutral; it's the meaning and momentum we attach to them that creates chaos. The patterns we repeat without questioning them—that's what keeps us stuck. That single flicker of awareness—the pause where you catch yourself—isn't small at all. It's the opening to everything different you've ever wanted to create.

Why the Moment That Matters Most Is the One We Skip

If the Choice Point is so powerful, why do so many people miss it?

Because it doesn't feel like a big, bold moment.

It doesn't announce itself with fireworks. It doesn't feel like a decision. It doesn't even feel particularly important—until you realize it's the exact spot where the future gets shaped.

What it *does* feel like is a tightening in your chest. A flush of heat in your face. A thought that flies in fast: *What did they mean by that? Maybe I should just drop it. Maybe I should say something right now before they think I'm weak.*

That's it. That's the doorway.

And your nervous system will try to slam it shut fast—because going through it requires presence. Choice. Power. And power, for many of us, hasn't always felt safe.

This is why people default to their old responses. Not because they want to—but because repetition feels safer than possibility.

The old response is automatic. It's efficient. It takes less effort and no reflection. It's been rehearsed so many times it plays like a song you can't get out of your head.

The Choice Point, on the other hand, is the unpracticed silence between the lyrics.

And when you've lived your life in noise, silence can feel like a threat instead of an invitation.

So instead of pausing, most people fill the space.

They send the reactive text. Over-explain the boundary. Launch the offer from scarcity. Ghost the opportunity they secretly wanted. Not because they're weak—but because they didn't yet know they had another option.

That's what the Choice Point offers: a different option.

One that requires courage. One that gets easier with practice. One that unlocks everything you say you want—but have struggled to actually let in.

And it starts with noticing.

Noticing doesn't sound sexy. But it's revolutionary when you've spent your life reacting. Because when you can notice the moment without letting it pull you under, you're no longer a slave to your history. You become someone who leads yourself into what's next—with clarity, with awareness, with power.

Making the Pause Big Enough to Choose Power

You don't expand this space by trying harder. You expand it by practicing differently.

Recognizing the Choice Point is a breakthrough—but expanding it is a practice. It's the difference between knowing the exit exists and actually taking the turn. The goal is to stretch that sliver of awareness into a space wide enough to hold a conscious decision, even in the moments when your nervous system is screaming to just react.

You're not trying to eliminate the response entirely. You're retraining your mind and body to choose something new—on purpose, with intention—before the old pattern sweeps you under again.

This is how you build that capacity:

1. Become a Pattern Tracker

Start with awareness. Look back over the past week and ask yourself:

- When did I react in a way I wasn't proud of?

- What typically sets me off?

- What physical sensations do I notice when it happens?

Be the observer, not the judge. You're collecting data on your own nervous system—not diagnosing it. Track the cues, the thoughts, the emotional flashpoints. The more familiar you become with your internal landscape, the easier it is to spot when you're about to veer off track.

2. Use Sensory Anchors to Interrupt the Spiral

When a trigger hits, your body floods with emotion. Your brain gets overtaken by a well-worn pattern. This is when the Choice Point is most vulnerable—because your system wants to do what it's always done.

Here's how you reclaim control:

- Step outside. Feel the ground beneath your feet.

- Place your hand on your chest and take three full breaths.

- Run cold water over your hands or grab something textured.

- Say out loud (or quietly in your head), *"I see what's happening. I can choose."*

Anchoring your awareness in the physical moment gives you just enough of a gap to remember—you don't have to go where this pattern wants to take you.

3. Ask a Higher-Self Question

In that gap—when the emotional wave hasn't yet taken over—drop in a question that shifts your vantage point:

- "What am I believing right now—and is it even true?"

- "What outcome do I want to create in this moment?"

- "What would the version of me I'm becoming

choose here?"

This isn't about silencing emotion. It's about shifting the driver's seat. Let your awareness take the lead—grounded in who you're becoming, not what you've survived.

Over time, this practice rewires your default settings. You won't just notice the Choice Point—you'll move through it with clarity, conviction, and power.

And when that happens? You stop bracing against your triggers and start building a life where you trust yourself to lead through them.

Responding From Power When Everything Wants You to React

It's one thing to recognize the Choice Point. It's another to embody it. To not just pause, but to pause with intention. To hold that space not as a delay tactic, but as an energetic doorway into who you are becoming.

The space you're learning to stretch? It's not passive. It's potent. It's where your future begins.

In fact, the most magnetic, grounded, and powerful people you admire—leaders who move with certainty, speak with clarity, and seem unshakable—aren't people who don't feel. They're people who've trained themselves to hold the Choice Point. To meet pressure with presence. To meet emotion with inquiry. To meet fear with aligned action.

And the difference that makes?

It's everything.

When you stop defaulting to your oldest reactions, you stop shrinking into your past. You stop making decisions from your trauma. You stop confusing urgency with clarity. You stop saying yes when you mean no. You stop over-explaining, over-apologizing, overcompensating.

You begin to respond from your center instead of your survival.

You begin to act like the version of you who doesn't abandon herself in the heat of the moment.

That's the power of this work.

And it's not something you master in theory—it's something you rehearse in the everyday moments that used to knock you out of alignment.

The Choice Point isn't reserved for big, dramatic events. It lives in the micro-moments. Like when your child pushes a boundary and you feel your voice rising—but you pause, breathe, and choose a calm presence instead. Or when a team member misses a deadline, and rather than spiraling into resentment, you lead the conversation with clarity and grace. Or when you catch yourself catastrophizing over one slow sales day, and instead of spinning out, you anchor back into trust.

These are the moments that shape who you become.

So, don't underestimate them.

Don't wait for a perfect scenario to practice. Start with what's in front of you today. Catch one tiny flicker of awareness. Interrupt one old pattern. Choose one new response.

Because every time you do?

You build self-trust.

You build emotional strength.

You build the internal safety that allows you to hold more power, more success, more visibility, more of the life you actually want.

And that kind of leadership? It doesn't just change your business or your relationships.

It changes your entire reality.

Becoming the Version Who Doesn't Default to the Old Script

This isn't about managing emotions. This is about mastering your ability to respond.

This is where your life is actually shaped—not in the big decisions, but in these subtle, repeated choices. Tiny decision points. Micro-choices. Split seconds where you can either fall back into the identity you've always carried—or lean forward into the one you're stepping into.

You don't need to be perfect. You don't need to pause every time. You just need to practice. Practice noticing. Practice pausing. Practice asking better questions. Practice choosing differently.

And every time you do—you don't just shift the moment.

You shift the trajectory.

You become someone who isn't ruled by old stories. Someone who isn't afraid of the trigger, the spiral, or the discomfort.

You become someone who leads herself through anything—

Not because life got easier, but because you stopped abandoning yourself when it got hard.

That's the moment your future stops echoing your past.

Not someday. Not once you're 'ready.'

But right now—

In the Choice Point.

Chapter Six

The Codes

You weren't meant to stay the same. You were meant to evolve, to rise, to remember who you are beneath all the layers the world told you to carry. You've always known this—quietly, deeply—but now you're ready to live it. Every page of this book has peeled something back—a belief, a story, a defense, a mask. You've confronted your patterns. You've sat with your triggers. You've questioned the rules you didn't even realize you were following. And in doing that, you've created space—not just to heal, but to expand.

Because this was never about fixing you. It's about freeing you. Freeing the version of you that's been buried under strategy, performance, and survival. The one who learned how to achieve but forgot how to receive. The one who stopped trusting her own power because she got too good at performing it. The one who can no longer afford to chase success if it means abandoning herself to get there.

That version of you isn't some distant future self. She's already here—quiet, steady, waiting beneath the noise. And this—right here—is where you let her lead. This is where we activate The Expansion Code™. Not a strategy. Not a step-by-step formula. A frequency. A remembering. A living embodiment of who you already are when you stop shrinking to fit inside old stories.

But you weren't ready for this part until now. You had to move through the fire first. Through the emotional loops you didn't know you were stuck in. Through the subconscious wiring that was quietly dictating your decisions. Through the Choice Point—the space where you finally stopped reacting and started responding with intention.

You had to remember that your triggers were never random. That your patterns weren't signs you were broken, but signals that you were surviving. That playing small wasn't weakness—it was protection. But now?

You're no longer here to protect the past. You're here to lead from your future. And that changes everything.

This is the shift from survival to expansion. From proving to presence. From holding it all together to finally holding all of you. This is The Expansion Code™—the seven truths that unlock the life and identity you were always meant to embody.

The 7 Truths of The Expansion Code™

The 7 Truths of The Expansion Code™ aren't just concepts. They're not mindset hacks, affirmations, or ideas to try on when life feels hard. These are codes—energetic anchors for the version of you who leads from wholeness, creates from truth, and receives without resistance. You've already cleared the clutter. You've interrupted the old loops. You've met yourself in the moments that used to unravel you. That's no small thing.

Now, you rise in these truths. Not as something you perform, but as the frequency you embody. These codes aren't something you memorize—they become the way you move. They rewire your identity from the inside out. Over time, expansion stops feeling like something to earn—and starts becoming the air you breathe.

1. Your Power Is Internal

You don't have to earn it.

You don't have to prove it.

And you sure as hell don't have to chase it.

Real power was never in the external. It was never in the results, the numbers, the praise, or the validation. It was never in being the loudest voice in the room—or the one who worked the hardest to be heard. It's what's underneath all of that. The calm. The knowing. The presence that doesn't flinch.

Power isn't something you "step into." It's what emerges when you stop performing.

When you stop trying to be more and start showing up as you.

No edits. No permission. No armor.

The moment you stop outsourcing your power—waiting for someone else to name it, crown it, validate it—you begin to access the kind of grounded authority that doesn't waver when circumstances shift.

It's not loud. It's not pushy.

It's the quiet inner stability that says:

I know who I am. And I don't have to prove it.

When power is internal, your strategy doesn't need to scream.

Your presence becomes the plan.

2. Identity Drives Everything

You can't outperform your identity.

No matter how hard you try. No matter how many strategies you master, goals you set, or mindset shifts you attempt—your life will always organize itself around who you believe you are.

Not who you say you are when you're feeling good. Not who you post about online.

But the quiet version you return to when no one's watching.

That version? That's the one creating your reality.

Your identity is the invisible script. It determines how much love you'll allow, how much ease you'll trust, how much success you'll receive before you start sabotaging it. It's not your desire that's driving the show—it's your self-concept.

You can change the external all you want.

You can switch niches, tweak your pricing, hire the best

coach in the world...

But if deep down you still see yourself as unworthy, behind, or not built for more—your reality will reflect that.

This is why change that sticks isn't cosmetic. It's cellular.

You don't just need a new plan.

You need to become someone new.

And that's not fake.

That's not bypassing.

That's reclaiming who you were before the world told you who to be.

Change the version of you that's holding the pen—and you stop rewriting the same chapter.

You start creating a new story entirely.

3. Your Reaction Is the Signal

Your emotional reactions aren't the problem.

They're the pattern interrupt. The portal. The moment your system says, "This is still alive inside of me."

Not because you're broken.

Not because you haven't healed enough.

But because your nervous system is doing exactly what it was wired to do—protect you.

That flash of anger. The urge to shut down. The spiral of doubt.

They're not signs you're failing.

They're signals—something unprocessed is asking to be seen.

This is where most people collapse—mistaking a trigger for a truth.

But when you meet that reaction with curiosity instead of shame, everything changes.

You're not reacting from the old story—you're listening to it.

You're not fighting the emotion—you're learning from it.

This is where the Trigger Response Method™ comes alive.

Not to make your reactions go away, but to show you what they're pointing to:

- A moment that was too much for your system to hold back then.

- A belief you absorbed before you knew you could question it.

- A part of you still trying to keep you safe—by keeping you small.

When you stop running from the reaction, you meet the root.

And when you meet the root, you reclaim your response.

This isn't about controlling your emotions.

It's about leading yourself through them—without abandoning who you are.

4. Make It Safe to Hold More

You don't keep what you don't feel safe holding.

Not love. Not money. Not visibility. Not ease.

Your nervous system is loyal—to you, but specifically to the version of you that's survived the longest. That version learned what was "safe" by watching what was familiar—not what was healthy, not what was expansive, just what kept you protected.

So if chaos was familiar, you'll recreate it.

If struggle earned love, you'll keep choosing hard.

If attention once led to pain, you'll shrink the second someone sees you.

And the worst part?

You'll call it self-sabotage. You'll beat yourself up for "getting in your own way."

But your system is actually doing what it believes will keep you alive.

This is why success doesn't feel how you thought it would.

The moment it shows up, the moment things get good... your body tenses.

Your breath shortens. Your mind starts scanning for what could go wrong.

It's not because you're ungrateful.

It's because you've never been taught how to feel safe in the having.

You don't outwork this. You rewire it.

You create new safety—not from the outside in, but from the inside out.

Breath by breath. Pattern by pattern. Moment by moment.

When your body learns that ease is safe, that receiving is safe, that being seen is safe—

that's when you stop dropping what you were always meant to hold.

5. Tell the Truth

Expansion doesn't begin when things feel good.
It begins the moment you get radically honest—with yourself.

Not honest like "I know I procrastinate sometimes."
Honest like "I'm choosing to avoid the thing I said I wanted, and I'm the only one responsible for that."

This is the code most people skip.
It asks more of you than mindset shifts or journal prompts ever will.
It asks you to look at the gap between what you say you want and how you're actually showing up—and to stop blaming anything outside of you for the difference.

Most people don't avoid growth because they're lazy.
They avoid it because being honest would require change.
And change would require responsibility.

It's easier to call it burnout than to admit you've been out of alignment.
Easier to blame the algorithm than to own that you've been playing small.

Easier to stay stuck in confusion than to admit you're afraid of what will happen if you finally go all in.

Let's call it what it is:

You won't expand if you're still lying to yourself.

You won't lead if you're still avoiding the mirror.

And you can't shift what you refuse to take responsibility for.

Radical honesty isn't about shame.

It's not about calling yourself out to feel bad.

It's about calling yourself forward—so you can finally move.

When you tell the truth, you stop leaking energy trying to pretend.

You stop performing.

You stop building momentum on a version of you that isn't real.

That's the moment everything realigns.

Because when you tell the truth, you dissolve the distortion.

And when the distortion clears, power flows in naturally.

This is what it means to live this code:

- Tell the truth about what you want.

- Tell the truth about what's in the way.

- Tell the truth about how you've been avoiding your own greatness.

Not with self-judgment.
But with self-respect.
When you take full responsibility for your life—
not part of it, not the curated version of it, not just the stuff that feels good—
you become unstoppable.
This is your expansion.
Not filtered. Not fixed. Just real.

6. Choose Differently

There's always a split second.
A micro-moment where the old reaction rises—and something in you knows: this is the fork in the road.
Do you spiral, lash out, shut down, over-explain, play small... again?
Or do you pause?
Feel the discomfort. Breathe through the urgency.
And choose a new path.

That moment—the Choice Point—is everything.

Not because it's flashy. Not because anyone else sees it.

But because it's the place where your future gets decided.

This is where the old story ends and a new one begins. Not in the big breakthrough, but in the 1,000 invisible choices you make when your system wants to go back—but you don't.

This is where the Trigger Response Method™ lives. Not in perfection. Not in knowing what to do every time.

But in pausing long enough to remember you have a choice.

Choose differently once—and you open the door.

Do it again—and you rewire the path.

Do it enough—and it becomes who you are.

Your next level won't come from waiting.

It will come from choosing—even when your voice shakes.

7. Lead Yourself First

You are the first person you'll ever lead.

And the one you lead the longest.

Before the clients.

Before the team.

Before the room.

Self-leadership isn't about having all the answers.
It's about how you move when no one's watching.

When fear rises, when pressure hits, when the old pattern begs you to shrink—do you follow it... or do you return to your truth?

This is the final code because it anchors all the rest.
Power. Identity. Safety. Choice.
None of it matters if you abandon yourself the second things get real.

You want to be a leader in the world?
Start by leading yourself through the moment that used to unravel you.

Not perfectly.

But powerfully.

And that begins with you.

Living the Code Daily

You don't become her in one decision.

You become her in the in-between.

In the quiet. In the ordinary.In the breath you take before reacting.

In the moment you choose not to spiral.

In the way you hold your energy when no one else would notice if you gave it away.

That's where the Expansion Code™ comes alive—Not as something you try to remember, but as something you return to.

Not as a script to follow, but a frequency you live.

Because it's easy to speak the language of expansion. It's easy to sound like growth. To talk the talk of leadership, power, and alignment.

But true embodiment is what shows up when no one's watching.

When the trigger hits. When the results haven't arrived yet—and you choose to hold the frequency anyway.

That's where embodiment begins—not in the spotlight, but in the shadows of your day, where no one else is watching.

The Expansion Code™ isn't something you visit in moments of motivation.It becomes your home.It's how you move through your day, your patterns, your emotions—differently.

When your launch isn't going as planned...

Your old self spirals. She grasps for control.

She starts overworking or undercharging to calm the panic in her chest.

But the version of you living by the Code pauses. She breathes.

She comes back to the truth: I don't chase results. I calibrate to who I'm becoming.

And from that energy, she recalibrates—not from panic, but from power.

She doesn't just recover—she reclaims the launch on her terms.

And it lands, not because she forced it, but because she stopped leaking power.

When you feel triggered by a client, a comment, or a moment...A comment catches you off guard. Your chest tightens. Your face flushes.

Old instincts rise—shut down, defend, over-explain.

But this time, you pause.

Your nervous system flares, but you don't bypass it.

You meet it.

You run it through the Trigger Response Method™.

You ask: What is this really about?

And suddenly, it's not just a reaction.

It's a signal. A portal.

This is something I'm ready to heal.

And when fear whispers that you're not ready…

The old identity wants to wait. Wants more certainty. Wants the guarantee.

But the expanded you?

She thanks the fear for trying to keep her safe—and she moves anyway.

Because she's not building a life from fear anymore. She's building it from faith.

From identity. From choice.

This is the embodiment of the Code.

It's not about doing more.

It's about choosing differently.

Not once, but again and again—until it becomes who you are.

Anchor Into Expansion

This isn't about mastering every hour.

It's about staying anchored in the moments that matter.

The ones that usually slip by unnoticed—the ones where identity is quietly shaped.

These three daily anchors will help you return to your power, your presence, and your truth—especially when things feel uncertain, uncomfortable, or unclear.

Morning: Lead the Day From Within

The moment you wake up, your mind may try to scan for problems—what's missing, what's late, what didn't happen fast enough yesterday.

But this is your first Choice Point.

The opportunity to return to your frequency before the world decides it for you.

Before you pick up your phone, before you respond to anyone else's urgency—drop into yourself.

Feel into the version of you who is leading your next level.

Not what she has. Not just what she does.

But how she feels. How she moves. What she no longer entertains.

Ask yourself:

- *Who am I becoming—and how would she move today?*

- *What energy do I want to lead with?*

- *What identity am I leaving behind right now?*

You're not just "starting your day with intention.

"You're stepping into alignment before momentum begins.

Midday: Interrupt the Spiral

At some point, the pattern will rise.

The doubt. The urgency. The comparison. The pressure to prove.

Maybe it happens during a tough conversation.

Maybe it's a failed post.

Maybe someone else is celebrating a win that makes you question your own.

This is the Choice Point.

This is your moment to come home to the version of you who doesn't chase safety—she *creates* it.

Pause. Breathe. Feel your body. Get honest. Ask:

- *What story am I about to act from?*

- *Is this coming from fear—or expansion?*

- *Is this my past leading... or my future?*

Even one breath between the pattern and the reaction is proof that you're becoming someone new.

That's embodiment. That's mastery. That's the Code in motion.

Evening: Rewire Through Reflection

Most people end their day with self-judgment—rehearsing what they didn't do, what they wish they said, how they "should've" shown up. But you're doing it differently now. You're rewiring your relationship with growth—by meeting yourself with compassion instead of criticism.

Ask yourself:

- Where did I show up in alignment with the Code today?

- Where did I slip into old patterns—and what did I learn?

- What will I choose differently tomorrow?

You are training your nervous system to feel safe in truth.

You are building an identity that doesn't collapse when things feel uncertain.

This is how expansion becomes sustainable—when you close the day with presence, not pressure.

These practices are your anchors. They're how you stay rooted when everything else wants you to react. It is how you build the kind of leadership that can hold more... without losing yourself in the process.

Because devotion to who you're becoming will always take you further than discipline ever could.

Because you weren't meant to chase alignment. You were meant to become it. And when you live the Code—not just speak it—you stop waiting to feel ready. You remember you already are.

You've already been doing the work—maybe without even realizing it.

The way you pause before reacting.

The way you notice what used to pull you out of yourself.

The way you're no longer willing to abandon what you know to be true just to keep the peace or be understood.

That's not just awareness. That's the embodiment.

This isn't about gathering more tools or proving how far you've come. It's about moving differently. Choosing from a deeper place. Living in alignment with the version of you who doesn't need to fight to be seen—because she already sees herself clearly. That's the shift you've been making—quietly, steadily, in the background of your everyday life.

Expansion doesn't mean resistance disappears. It means you've stopped letting it dictate your decisions. You'll still feel the pull of old patterns. You'll still hear the voice that wants to keep you small. But now, you recognize it for what it is: a leftover version of you—not a truth you have to follow.

You pause. You breathe. And you move anyway.

Not because you feel fully ready, but because you trust yourself to handle what comes next.

This is what it means to lead from identity.

To hold who you're becoming—even in the moments that once unraveled you.

To choose presence when it would be easier to disconnect.

To choose power when the familiar option is to shrink.

It's not about getting it perfect. It's about getting honest. Over and over again.

You don't need a better plan.

You need a deeper relationship with yourself. And the more often you choose from that place, the more natural it becomes. Expansion stops feeling like something you chase—and starts becoming the new normal you build your life around.

This is your turning point.

Not loud. Not rushed. Not performative.

Rooted. Clear. Unshakable.

Now that you've remembered your power, it's time to rebuild everything from that place.

To reclaim the beliefs, identities, and patterns that shaped your limits—so you can rise beyond them.

The code has been revealed—but a code is only powerful when it's lived.

And this is where you begin living it.

Chapter Seven

Rewrite the Script: Identity Is the Origin of It All

You've learned how to perform.

To show up. To execute. To deliver.

Maybe you've mastered the calendar, the strategy, the team management, the launch cycle.

Or maybe you've climbed the ladder, led departments, hit your KPIs, and checked every box that was supposed to lead to fulfillment.

No one warns you about this part:

If the identity behind the action hasn't shifted, none of it sticks.At some point, it starts to feel like you're holding it all together with a threadbare version of who you used to be.

You can walk into a boardroom with a title, but if you still see yourself as someone who has to prove their value to belong—you'll leave that meeting questioning everything you said.

You can lead a successful team or company, but if your internal belief system says "I have to overwork to earn this," you'll keep piling pressure on yourself until the success becomes unsustainable.

And over time, that pressure doesn't just drain your energy—it chips away at your confidence, leaving even your biggest wins feeling empty.

I once worked with a client who had just hit her biggest month in business—financially, she was thriving. But the moment things started to feel good, she began picking apart the details. She redid emails that had already worked. Rewrote messaging that was already converting. Not because it wasn't working—but because ease still felt suspicious to her. Her nervous system didn't feel safe holding the success she'd created. And so she unconsciously created resistance—not out of self-sabotage, but because her identity hadn't caught up to her results.

This isn't about confidence. It's about congruence. You can be confident in a room and still question your value the moment you leave.

Congruence is what makes that confidence last.

It's about aligning the way you see yourself with the level you're being called into.

Because your actions will always submit to your self-concept.

So even when you're doing everything "right," if the identity underneath still believes it's not enough—you'll sabotage, stall, or overcompensate.

That's why Expansion isn't just a decision—it's a code.

And Code 6 lives here: in the moment you choose to stop performing who you've been, and start embodying who you've decided to become.

And if you don't update the version of you that's running the show behind the scenes, you'll keep snapping back to familiar patterns—no matter how much success you create on paper.

This is the real root work.

Because until your identity feels safe in success—safe in visibility, rest, ease—you'll unconsciously create friction to justify your old beliefs.

No strategy, system, or performance review can fix what identity work must heal.

Until your identity feels worthy and grounded in who you're becoming, you'll unconsciously sabotage, shrink, or stall the second you rise.

So if it feels like you're constantly hitting a ceiling...

If the wins don't feel as satisfying as they should...

If you feel like you're "doing all the right things" and still wondering why it's not landing—

You're not broken. You're just outgrowing the version of you that was built to survive in a smaller space.

It's time to lead from the inside out.

Not from pressure.

Not from performance.

But from the truth of who you've always been.

Where Belief Becomes Blueprint

If your identity sets the tone, your beliefs write the script.

Most people try to change their outcomes by adjusting surface behaviors—working harder, tweaking routines, switching jobs, hiring coaches, downloading new tools. But the real question isn't *what are you doing?* What *do you believe is possible for someone like you?*

Because if, underneath it all, you still believe you're only valuable when you're achieving—then no title, salary, or success will ever feel like enough.

When your nervous system links ease with laziness, chaos becomes the default—because chaos feels productive. It feels like you're earning something, even when you're exhausted.

If you've internalized that being fully seen comes with risk, you'll find ways to shrink—on Zoom calls, in boardrooms, in your content—even when you're the most qualified person in the room.

Beliefs are invisible architects.

They shape your decisions, your responses, your risks—and most importantly, your capacity to receive.

And the thing about beliefs?

They don't have to be true to be powerful.

They just have to be repeated enough that your brain accepts them as fact.

Which is why this next phase of your expansion isn't just about learning something new.

It's about unlearning everything that told you who you had to be in order to succeed.

It's about updating the stories you didn't even realize you were living by.

So if you've ever wondered:

- Why does success feel so hard to hold?

- Why do I always pull back just before the next big leap?

- Why do I keep recreating the same results, no matter how much I grow?

The answer isn't in your effort. It's in your internal blueprint.

Because until you rewire the belief system running the show, you'll keep reaching for new outcomes with an outdated operating system.

And that's exactly what we're here to shift.

The Beliefs You Never Meant to Choose

You didn't consciously choose the beliefs shaping your reality. They weren't decisions. They were downloads. Picked up in fleeting moments you didn't even realize were shaping you. Absorbed from the energy of rooms you grew up in. Modeled by the people you trusted, feared, admired—or depended on for love. Reinforced through repetition until they stopped sounding like stories and started feeling like truth.

They sound like protection. Like logic. Like wisdom wrapped in fear.

"Don't get too comfortable or you'll lose it."

"Slow down and you'll fall behind."

"If you stand out, people will pull away."

"If you succeed, they'll expect more—and you'll disappoint them."

They don't yell. They whisper. But those whispers become the script. They shape what you say yes to. What you avoid. What you think you're allowed to receive.

The job you turn down because it feels too big. The opportunity you delay because you're "not ready." The price you lower because you don't want to be "too much." The truth you water down so you don't ruffle feathers.

And this is the part that keeps most people stuck—not because they're incapable, but because they're still living by rules they never questioned.

These aren't just beliefs. They are survival codes. And even when they hurt you, your nervous system holds onto them—because familiar still feels safer than free.

But here's the shift: Beliefs don't need to be true to have power. They just need to go unchallenged.

So if you're ready to create something new in your external world, you can't just look forward. You have to look inward. You have to ask:

What belief am I still living by that no longer belongs to the future I'm building?

Because real transformation doesn't come from better plans. It comes from braver questions.

And the moment you stop organizing your identity around an outdated version of who you were told to be? You get to become someone you never thought you were allowed to be.

Rewiring Begins in the Micro-Moment

Change doesn't begin when you sit down to journal. It begins in the moment your voice catches in your throat before speaking up in the meeting. When your stomach tightens as you raise your prices. When you hesitate to share your idea because it feels just a little too bold. These are the real battlegrounds of belief—the quiet, in-between moments where your past identity tries to reclaim control.

This is where most transformation work falls short. It focuses on the ritual—the journaling, the affirmations, the vision board mantras—without addressing the root. If your body doesn't believe the new identity, it will reject it no matter how often you say it. Affirmations only go so far when your nervous system is still bracing for the fallout of being seen. Real change happens not when you say something new—but when your body finally feels safe enough to believe it.

Rewiring doesn't begin with positivity. It begins with *presence.*

You have to be willing to witness the moment your old beliefs want to lead—and interrupt the pattern before it becomes automatic. You don't have to know exactly what to say. You don't have to fix the whole story. You just need to pause long enough to choose again.

That's the moment the Expansion Code activates. The instant where Code 6 whispers: choose different-ly—not because it's easy, but because it's aligned.

It might sound like: *"That's the old belief. I don't follow that anymore."* Or: *"This fear doesn't belong to who I am becoming."* Or even: *"This reaction is familiar—but it's not the only option."*

It's not about feeling fearless. It's about *noticing* the fear, and choosing anyway.

That's how new beliefs are built. Not in isolation, but in real life—in the day-to-day decisions where your past identity would have pulled you back, and instead, you stayed present. It's the small moments that matter most. Not because they're dramatic, but because they're honest. Real. Raw. And rewiring doesn't need drama—it needs devotion.

Every time you choose from presence instead of programming, you begin to build a new pathway in your brain. And the more often you walk that path, the stronger it becomes. Until one day, the old beliefs feel less believable. The old stories feel less seductive. The old reactions don't feel like home anymore.

This is how you become someone new. Not all at once—but one pattern interrupt at a time.

Prove It to Your Brain, Not the World

Your brain doesn't change based on what you hope for. It changes based on what you *prove.*

And right now, it's been gathering evidence for the same old beliefs—some of which you didn't even choose. Beliefs passed down through family, culture, or past experiences. Beliefs that say you have to struggle to succeed, that rest equals laziness, or that visibility makes you unsafe. And because your brain is designed to filter reality through what it already believes, you will continue to find confirmation of those stories—unless you start offering it something new.

This is where conscious rewiring begins. You don't just *think* differently—you teach your brain to see differently.

Start by asking yourself: *What if I could build evidence for a different story?*

If the old belief is *"I always mess it up,"* look for the moments you didn't.

The times you followed through.

The times you recovered.

The times it worked out.

If the old story is *"People don't see me,"* start documenting every time someone did. Every comment, every message, every compliment, every glance of recognition. Show your brain the truth it's been trained to miss.

This isn't about erasing your pain or denying what shaped you—it's about expanding your perspective. The version of you who feels stuck is viewing life through the lens of survival. But that's not the whole story. There are already moments in your past that reflect power, clarity, and expansion. You just haven't been taught to name them as proof—yet.

Your next-level identity isn't a fantasy. It's built on real, lived experiences that your brain has filtered out in favor of the familiar struggle. But the more often you name the moments where you chose courage, showed up aligned, or felt grounded in your power—even for a breath—the more you rewire what your nervous system accepts as normal.

This is how you begin to let go of the old narrative—not by rejecting your past, but by outgrowing the version of you who needed it. You're not pretending the pain didn't exist. You're proving it's no longer the only story worth telling.

Make this a daily practice. Track your evidence like it matters—because it does. Screenshot the unexpected compliment. Note the decision you made from self-trust instead of fear. Remember the day you felt ease, even if nothing changed externally. These aren't just feel-good moments. They are neurological shifts—tiny, powerful affirmations that your reality is already changing.

You're not just thinking new thoughts. You're re-training your brain to live a new truth. And when you do that enough, your identity begins to catch up.

Let the Future Feel Like Home

Here's the truth about why people sabotage the exact success they've been working for:

It's not because they're incapable.

It's because the new identity still feels unfamiliar.

Your subconscious is wired to protect what feels *normal*—not what feels exciting or expansive. And if your old identity has been wrapped in struggle, self-doubt, or playing small, then anything outside of that—even if it's everything you've ever wanted—will feel like a threat.

That's why people revert.

They get the opportunity, and they ghost it. They finally feel seen, and they shrink. They reach the next level, and they panic.

Not because they don't want it—but because part of them doesn't feel safe *having* it.

The solution isn't to work harder.

It's to make your next level feel like home.

You have to normalize the new identity—not just in your mind, but in your body. You do this through repetition, exposure, and presence. You start living as the version of you who already has it... not when it feels easy, but especially when it feels uncomfortable.

That might mean walking into a room like you belong before anyone validates that you do.

It might mean raising your hand in the meeting even while your heart races.

It might mean sitting in stillness when your old self would have sprinted into overworking.

These aren't performative acts. They're nervous system recalibrations. You're retraining your body to feel safe in expansion.

To feel at home in visibility.

To stop bracing for failure when things start going well.

Every time you choose presence over programming, you're practicing the code. Not by force—but by frequency.

That's what rewiring really is: the consistent, embodied decision to live in alignment with who you're becoming.

This is how you collapse the gap between who you've been and who you're becoming—not by waiting for the new identity to feel natural, but by choosing it *until* it does.

The more you show up that way, the less you'll flinch.

The less you flinch, the more your body adjusts.

And eventually? You stop faking it. You *become* it.

You don't have to force belief. You have to *familiarize* it.

Because once your subconscious feels safe in your new identity, it stops fighting for your old one.

Identity Is The Real Work

By now, you're seeing it clearly: the thoughts that were never truly yours, the beliefs that were inherited, the identities you've outgrown. You've uncovered the quiet patterns running beneath the surface—shaping your choices, distorting your confidence, and keeping you tethered to a version of yourself that no longer fits.

This is your reclamation.

The moment you stop waiting for something outside of you to shift—and start becoming the one who rewrites the script.

Change doesn't happen through force. It happens through frequency.

Through subtle recalibration. Through choosing to live from truth instead of survival.

It means you stop reacting from old fears and start responding from embodied clarity.It means your moves are no longer dictated by past programming—but aligned with who you've decided to become.

And that decision? You don't make it once. You make it again and again.Not perfectly. Not loudly. But consistently—until the new identity no longer feels like a stretch and starts feeling like home.

This is what it looks like when the Expansion Code comes alive.Not something you turn to in moments of inspiration—but a way of moving through the world. A daily embodiment.

A living declaration that says: *I choose differently now.*

Breakthroughs will open the door—but your life is built in the moments that follow.

In the quiet, courageous decision to not abandon yourself.

To stay present.

To remember: *I lead from who I'm becoming—not from who I've been.*

This is where the shift becomes sustainable.

Not through intensity, but through integration.

Not by chasing the next breakthrough, but by embodying what you already know.

You're not becoming someone else.

You're returning to someone you were never meant to forget.

And every time you choose from *that* place—you're not just leading your life.

You're redefining it.

Chapter Eight

Where Leadership Really Begins

*A*s you expand into a new identity, you'll be called to lead—first yourself, then others.

Because true expansion doesn't stop at self-discovery. It asks you to carry that truth forward.

Lead Yourself First

Leadership has nothing to do with titles, follower counts, or how loudly you speak. It's about how you move when no one is watching. How you respond when there's no applause, no certainty, and no guarantees. True leadership begins in the spaces where no one is clapping, but you keep going anyway.

Most people misunderstand what leadership really is.

They think leadership is about being the most visible, the most polished, or the most experienced. But it's not about gaining approval or having all the answers. It's about how you lead when the path is unclear, the pressure is rising, and your next step requires more self-trust than certainty.

Real leadership—the kind that moves people without needing to convince them—starts in the quiet. In the tension. In the stretch between who you've been and who you're becoming. That's where your power is tested. And that's where it's earned.

You don't become a leader when everything feels solid. You become a leader when everything is shifting—and you choose to move anyway.

I once worked with a client, Alisha, during a season where everything looked successful on the outside. Her offers were selling. Her audience was growing. Her brand was beautifully built. But underneath it all, she felt like a fraud. Every time her visibility increased, she would quietly retreat—skipping livestreams, softening her message, disappearing for weeks. Not because she feared failure, but because she didn't feel ready to lead.

Not while she still had doubts. Not while she was still figuring things out behind the scenes.

"I know people see me as successful," she said during one of our calls. "But what if I'm not who they think I am?"

That moment shifted everything. Because leadership isn't about being ready. It's about being willing. Willing to hold yourself through the wobble. Willing to rise before it's comfortable. Willing to be seen, even when your voice shakes.

Leadership isn't a destination you reach once everything's perfect. It's a decision you make in real time—especially when it's hard. Alisha didn't need more strategy. She needed to reconnect with the version of herself who could hold the weight of being seen and still stand in her truth. The version of her who could lead—not just when it felt good—but when it mattered most.

This kind of leadership isn't about performance or polish. It's about presence. It's about honoring who you're becoming, not who you think you need to be to keep everyone comfortable. It doesn't begin with managing perception. It begins with building internal safety—and choosing to move from that place, even when it's unfamiliar, even when it's messy, even when the easier choice would be to shrink.

That's the kind of leadership that lasts.

Integration Is the Initiation

This is where it starts to get real.

Leadership isn't a title. It's not how many people follow you or how loud your message gets.

Leadership is how you carry yourself in the in-between.

It's how you respond when doubt creeps in. It's how you hold your power when something doesn't go as planned. It's how you move when no one is clapping, when results feel slow, when your message lands in silence instead of praise.

Insight is no longer enough.

This is the moment in your journey where awareness becomes embodiment.

Where insight becomes integration.

You've done the excavation. You've uncovered the triggers, the patterns, the protective payoffs. You've rewritten the script.

Now the question becomes:

Can you live it?

Because leadership isn't about never getting activated again. It's about what you do *once you are.*

Can you pause before reacting?

Can you stay with yourself instead of abandoning your voice to make someone else comfortable?

Can you let your body feel the fear and still choose alignment?

That's real power.

And it's subtle.

It's the decision to stay open in a room where you once would have shrunk.It's choosing to speak clearly instead of over-explaining. It's letting yourself be fully seen—even when part of you still wants to run.

Most people don't realize how often they're out-sourcing their leadership. Not to a mentor or strategy—but to old parts of themselves that are still trying to be liked. Still trying to belong. Still trying to avoid being misunderstood or judged.

That's why true leadership requires deep integration. It's not performative—it's embodied. It lives in your nervous system. It lives in the way you breathe before you speak, in the way you hold your posture when your idea is questioned, in the way you trust yourself to be with discomfort without collapsing into it.

I had a client—let's call her Ana—who built a wildly successful company but kept holding herself back from stepping into the spotlight of her own brand. She was a brilliant strategist, but behind the scenes, she always deferred the visibility to others. When we traced the thread back, we found an old wound: growing up, she'd been taught that being outspoken made her "too much." That her power made people uncomfortable. That leadership came with loss.

So every time Ana got close to claiming her space, that belief would whisper, *Don't be too big. Don't make people uncomfortable. Don't lead too boldly or you'll lose love.*

She thought she had a confidence issue. What she really had was a nervous system still running an outdated definition of safety.

What changed everything wasn't another marketing plan or speech training. It was this: learning to lead herself through the discomfort. Learning to stay with the version of her that felt like she might be "too much" and breathe instead of shrink. Speak instead of edit. Lead instead of wait for permission.

And once she did?

Her voice didn't just land differently. *She* did.

This is where you take what you have learned and really put it into practice.

Not just seeing the trigger—but holding your center when it flares. Not just naming your power—but owning it when it would be easier to give it away. Not just rewriting the pattern—but showing up as someone who no longer lives inside it.

Because this is the moment where you stop simply *knowing* what's possible—and start *leading* like it.

When the Old Identity Tries to Lead

The old patterns don't disappear just because you've grown.

They soften. They get quieter. They lose their grip. But sometimes, in moments of uncertainty or stretch, they still whisper.

Don't say too much.

Make it easier for everyone else.

You're not ready yet.

This might be too big for you.

And if you're not careful, those whispers start to sound like wisdom.

That's what makes leadership in the real world so different from leadership in theory. It's not about being unshakable—it's about knowing what to do *when you are shaken.*

It's about hearing the whisper of an old belief and deciding it doesn't get to make the next move.

It's about feeling the pull to people-please or downplay or delay—and choosing presence instead.

One of the biggest lies the old patterns sell you is that you have to *feel completely ready* before you act differently. But embodied leadership doesn't wait for the fear to disappear. It moves *with it,* rooted in a deeper truth:

I am not my reaction. I am the one choosing the response.

So how do you lead when the old version of you still tries to take the mic?

You slow it all down.

You notice what's happening—without spiraling into shame.

You pause long enough to ask:

"Is this truth—or is this an echo?" "Is this mine—or is this a memory?" "Is this the leader in me—or the part still trying to earn safety?"

This is where the Choice Point becomes a leadership practice. And this is where you begin to embody the Expansion Code—right here, in the pause. Where Code 6—*Choose Differently*—meets Code 7—*Lead Yourself First.*

Because it's not about waiting for the fear to leave. It's about deciding that who you're becoming leads now.

Because you're no longer just interrupting the pattern for your own healing—you're doing it to lead others better. You're doing it because the work you're here to do in the world *requires* you to hold yourself differently.

And sometimes that means making the brave choice while the old narrative is still talking.

Not waiting until you *feel* confident to raise your rates, pitch the room, hold the boundary. But acting from the part of you that *knows*—even if a different part is still catching up.

Because leadership isn't clean. It's not always poised and polished. Sometimes it's gritty. Sometimes your voice shakes. Sometimes you lead *with the whisper still present.*

But the difference is—*you're the one in charge now.*

That whisper might still echo, but it doesn't get to drive. It doesn't get to choose how you move. And every time you lead through it, it gets quieter. Every time you stay with yourself instead of abandoning who you're becoming, you prove to your system that the old story isn't the whole story anymore.

And that's when something deeper settles in.

You stop trying to "fix" the parts of you that still get scared.You start trusting that you can hold them—and still lead powerfully.

That's real leadership. Not perfection. Not performance.

Presence. Power. Integrity.

Let Go of Being Liked

There's a quiet grief that comes with leadership no one talks about.

The grief of being misunderstood. Of not being everyone's favorite anymore. Of realizing that the more honest, grounded, and powerful you become—the more likely it is that someone will misinterpret you, pull away from you, or project onto you the very thing they haven't yet faced in themselves.

This is the part of leadership that unravels people the most.

Not the decisions. Not the workload. Not the pressure.

But the emotional discomfort of not being liked for doing what's right.

If you've built your identity around being the one who makes everyone else feel good, this part will feel like a death. Because the moment you start honoring your truth, your time, your capacity—you'll notice. People who benefited from your self-abandonment will fall away. People who loved your softness may not know what to do with your strength.

And if you're not anchored in who you are, you'll try to shrink again to keep the peace.

But peace built on your silence is not peace. Connection that costs you your truth is not connection. And leadership that avoids being seen as "too much" is not leadership—it's performance.

The people-pleasing version of you can't lead a powerful life. She can build a business. She can grow a brand. She can attract approval. But she will never feel free.

Because her power is still tied to perception.

Real leadership means knowing that being liked is not the goal.

Being honest is.

Being whole is.

Being in integrity is.

There's a kind of liberation that comes when you realize: you can disappoint someone and still be a good person. You can be misread and not bend yourself into a version that's easier to digest. You can speak with certainty and not need everyone in the room to agree.

Because the version of you who's here to lead doesn't trade power for approval anymore.

She leads herself first.

That's the Expansion Code in action.

Not to impress. Not to be perfect. But because she knows her truth is stronger than the need to be understood.

And when you let go of needing to be liked, you unlock something even more magnetic: trust.

People might not always like what you say. But they'll trust that you mean it.

They might not always agree with your decisions. But they'll respect how you make them.

They might not always see you clearly. But *you* will.

And that clarity? That integrity?

That's the kind of leadership that moves people. That changes companies. That builds legacies.

It doesn't shout. It doesn't beg. It doesn't chase.

It anchors.

Self-Leadership Is the Standard

Self-leadership isn't a vague concept.

It's not just about showing up with confidence or saying the right things in a team meeting.

It's about identifying the exact places in your life where you've been waiting—stalling—looping.

Then choosing to lead yourself through them before asking the world to follow your vision.

It starts where it's least glamorous and most honest.

Leading yourself first might look like:

- Making the financial decision you've been avoiding.

- Having the uncomfortable conversation that keeps circling your mind.

- Honoring the structure you said you'd commit to—even when no one's watching.

- Saying no to things you used to say yes to out of guilt, fear, or old programming.

- Launching the program you've been sitting on—not when it's perfect, but when you feel the edge of your growth asking you to go.

You don't need a five-year vision to lead.

You need to take ownership of the places where you've been playing small while calling it strategy.

You need to stop waiting for conditions to feel safe and start choosing to move while it still feels edgy.

This is the code in motion.

Code 7: Lead Yourself First.

Not in theory—but in real time, where it counts.

This is how leadership gets anchored.

Not in a title.

Not in a launch.

But in the moments you choose to follow through before the clarity comes.

When you stop waiting to feel qualified—and start honoring the part of you that already knows.

Because self-leadership isn't a bonus skill.

It's the blueprint for everything else you want to hold.

Ask yourself:

- Where am I still asking for permission before I move?

- Where do I wait for clarity instead of creating it?

- Where do I keep handing my power to circumstances instead of stepping forward with what's available right now?

Leading yourself first means you stop outsourcing responsibility for your next level.

It means you stop waiting for your nervous system to feel perfectly safe before you act.

It means you stop needing a guarantee before you show up like you're already the one.

Because no matter how strategic or gifted or magnetic you are—

if you won't lead yourself through the tension,
you'll never feel safe holding the expansion you're calling in.

You can't lead others—clients, teams, communities—into deeper levels of ownership if you won't go there yourself.

Leadership starts behind the scenes.

In the mornings where you want to numb.
In the decision you've been dragging your feet on.
In the boundary you know you need to hold, even if your voice shakes.
In the moment you notice the fear rise—and choose to move anyway.

This is the kind of leadership that makes you magnetic.
Not because you're polished.
But because you're consistent with yourself.
Because you lead with integrity behind closed doors.
Because you live your work before you teach it.

That's what makes you unshakable—
not the absence of fear,
but the presence of follow-through.

And when you live like that?

You don't have to tell people you're a leader.
They'll feel it.

Because you're already leading the one person who matters most: you.

The life you want won't be led by who you've been. It will be led by who you're willing to become—moment by moment, choice by choice, day by day.

Chapter Nine

From Radical Responsibility to Real Freedom

There was a time I lied to myself more than anyone else ever could.

Not with words, but with stories. With performances. With just enough awareness to convince myself I was doing the work—while avoiding the parts that actually mattered.

I told myself I was fine when I wasn't. I pretended I was over things I hadn't even begun to process. I called it "alignment" when I was actually just avoiding the next level because it scared me.

I didn't want to tell the truth—because truth requires change. And change requires responsibility.

Owning that I was the one holding myself back?

That meant I had to do something about it. It meant I could no longer point to strategy gaps or timing or other people's expectations as the reason I wasn't where I wanted to be.

And for a long time, I wasn't ready for that.

Because truth always asks for something in return: the illusion of comfort, the drama that distracts, the version of you that got really good at pretending things were fine.

This is what revealed itself through the work:

Radical responsibility is the portal.

It's the moment everything starts to shift—not because you've figured it all out, but because you've stopped lying about why you haven't.

This isn't the kind of responsibility that comes with shame or self-punishment. It's not about judging your past or carrying the weight of the world on your back. It's about reclaiming your role as the one in charge of your life.

They say they want change—but rarely want to become the version of themselves that change requires.

They want the breakthrough without the breakdown.

The clarity without the confrontation.

The power—without taking ownership of where they've been giving it away.

Radical responsibility is the line.

The invisible one that separates those who spin in the same stories year after year... from those who actually shift.

And it always starts with truth.

The moment you stop avoiding what you know.

The moment you stop waiting for circumstances to change before you decide to.

The moment you stop telling yourself you're unclear—when really, you're afraid of what the clarity might require.

That's the moment everything begins to move—not because you've forced a breakthrough, but because you've finally stopped resisting the truth. The trigger that once sent you spiraling becomes a teacher. The doubt that felt like a setback becomes a doorway. The vision you've been holding onto stops feeling hypothet-ical—and starts taking shape as something inevitable.

But it can't happen without honesty.

Honesty so deep it unravels the versions of you that survived on half-truths.

Honesty so grounded it doesn't need to perform or prove.

Honesty that clears the static—so you can finally hear yourself again.

That's the foundation this work is built on.

Not control. Not perfection.

Ownership.

TRM in Motion: Own It or Repeat It

What most people overlook about growth is this: aware-ness opens the door—but it's ownership that moves you through it.

You can know your triggers, unpack your childhood patterns, name every belief you've inherited—and still stay stuck if you don't take responsibility for shifting them.

That's where The Trigger Response Method™ comes in. It gives you a tool—but you still have to use it. And using it requires something deeper than insight. It requires the willingness to see that if you created the pattern... you also hold the power to change it.

Responsibility is the bridge between knowing better and doing differently.

It's the moment the Expansion Code™ shifts from theory to embodiment.

Because the Code isn't something you memorize. It's something you practice—every time you choose to respond from truth instead of reactivity.

When your system gets activated, you have a choice. You can collapse into the story—or you can use the trigger as data. Not as proof that you're failing, but as feedback that something inside you wants to be seen.

This is why TRM is more than a method—it's a mirror.

It shows you what's really running the show. It reveals what's still unresolved. And most importantly, it hands you back the pen.

Because once you recognize your reactions aren't random, you stop feeling like a victim to them. You start seeing them as invitations. Portals. Opportunities to pause and shift from unconscious loops into conscious leadership.

And that doesn't just change your emotional life—it changes your results.

You show up differently in business. You communicate more clearly in relationships. You stop chasing strategy and start aligning with self-trust.

The moment you stop outsourcing your reactions and start owning your responses, you become the kind of person who can hold expansion—not just talk about it.

That's what makes TRM powerful. Not because it makes you perfect. But because it puts you back in the driver's seat.

Not once. But every single time it matters most.

I've worked with clients who could map every trigger and name every pattern—and still stay stuck. Not because they didn't understand, but because they were waiting for the fear to go away before they made a move.

One client, for example, had done all the inner work on paper. She knew why she over-explained. She could track the original wound. But every time a client questioned her price, she froze. Because knowing the trigger wasn't the same as holding herself through it.

That's where the real power of TRM lives—not in eliminating your reactions, but in learning how to hold your center when they hit. Not in waiting for the wobble to disappear, but in anchoring your truth while it's still present.

Stop Outsourcing Your Power

If you feel stuck—emotionally, financially, creatively—it's not because you don't know enough.

It's because you're still unconsciously waiting for something outside of you to shift first.

This is one of the most common places people get trapped. They think they're doing the work, but really, they're still negotiating with life. Still hoping the clarity will come *before* they move. Still waiting for permission to act, for circumstances to get easier, for someone to show up and validate that they're ready.

Let's be honest,

Every place you're waiting is a place you've handed away your power.

That might sound harsh, but it's also incredibly freeing—because it means you can take it back.

Start here:

Look at the area of your life that feels most frustrating right now.

Maybe it's money.

Maybe it's visibility.

Maybe it's confidence, consistency, momentum.

Now ask:

What am I secretly waiting for?

Are you waiting for someone to believe in you?

Waiting for proof that it will work?

Waiting for the fear to go away?

Waiting until it's perfect before you let yourself begin?

Flip it.

If you fully believed the outcome was your responsibility—what would you do differently today?

Most people never ask that question. Because it requires them to face the real reason they're stuck.

Not because they're not good enough.

Not because they don't know what to do.

But because they're afraid to own that it's up to them.

When you take radical responsibility, you stop needing the conditions to be ideal before you act. You stop playing the waiting game. You stop outsourcing momentum to the algorithm, your coach, your bank account, or your past.

You lead.

You make the move. You have the conversation. You launch the thing. You take the first step—not because you feel ready, but because you've decided to stop waiting.

That's how you shift.

Not by finding the "right" time.

But by becoming the person who no longer waits for it.

The Power of Owning It All

I used to think taking full responsibility would be exhausting.

I thought it would make everything heavier—like the weight of my entire life would suddenly fall on my shoulders.

But what I didn't realize was that I was already carrying that weight.

Just in a different way.

I was carrying the energy of pretending.

Of blaming things I couldn't control.

Of telling myself stories that made my stuckness feel safer than the truth.

I said I was doing everything I could.

That I was showing up.

That I was just waiting for the right moment, the right sign, the right "clarity."

But deep down, I knew I wasn't being honest with myself.

I was avoiding the parts of me that felt behind.

Avoiding the dreams that scared me.

Avoiding the reality that the only thing standing between where I was and where I wanted to be… was me.

And the day that changed was the day I stopped pretending.

I sat with the question:

What if nothing outside of me is the problem?

What if it's just me—avoiding the truth because I didn't want to be responsible for what came next?

That question cracked something open.

It wasn't dramatic. There was no breakdown or revelation. Just a quiet decision that I was done lying to myself.

I was done calling it burnout when it was misalignment.

Done blaming the algorithm when I hadn't been consistent.

Done saying I wasn't ready when I was just afraid of what would happen if I finally went all in.

That moment changed everything. Because I stopped outsourcing my power. And started using it.

From that point on, everything in my business and life began to reflect a deeper level of truth. Not because circumstances suddenly got easier, but because I was no longer fighting my own knowing.

I launched offers with clarity—not because I was certain they'd sell, but because I was certain I was aligned.

I set boundaries without guilt. I showed up before I felt perfectly "ready." I let my truth be louder than my fear.

And I became someone I could trust.

That's what radical responsibility *actually* does. It's not about hustling harder or holding everything alone.

It's about reclaiming the parts of you you've given away—bit by bit, lie by lie, avoidance by avoidance.

It's the most freeing thing you'll ever do.

Because you don't have to wait anymore.

Not for the perfect timing.

Not for someone else's permission.

Not for the fear to disappear.

You get to lead.

You get to move forward—not because everything is figured out, but because you've finally decided to own all of it. The wins, the mess, the patterns, the power.

This is what real change is built on.

Not the surface-level shifts. Not the performative growth. But the quiet, grounded decision to tell the truth—even when no one else is watching.

From Knowing to Living

Radical responsibility isn't just something you practice when it's convenient. It's how you anchor the entire Expansion Code™ in your life.

Because everything changes the moment you stop outsourcing your power.

When you stop waiting for certainty.

When you stop performing growth—and start embodying it.

You've already done the inner work. You've faced your patterns, your reactions, your beliefs. You've opened space in your system to hold more—not just intellectually, but energetically. And now, this is where it all gets real.

This is where it moves from concept to commitment.

From knowing to living.

From awareness to ownership.

And that's what the Expansion Code™ is all about.

It's not something you remember once in a while. It's not a list you revisit when things fall apart. It becomes how you see. How you decide. How you move.

You live the Code when you take full ownership of your reactions instead of blaming your environment.

You live it when you tell the truth—even when it's uncomfortable.You live it when you lead yourself—especially when no one else would know if you didn't.

This is the moment it clicks: The Expansion Code™ isn't something you're trying to achieve. It's already in you.

The more honest you are, the more clearly you see it.

The more responsible you become, the more power you access.

The more you live it, the more it rewires who you are—without needing to try so hard.

And that's the point.

When you let the Code become who you are...You stop searching for the next answer.

You realize you've been it all along.

Chapter Ten

Staying in the Work When It's Not Easy

They never come when it's convenient.

Not when everything is flowing, not when your nervous system feels calm and confident, and certainly not when you're riding a wave of clarity and momentum. They arrive in the quiet spaces—in the stretch between who you've been and who you're becoming. In the silence after a bold move. In the delay before the result.

The contraction.

The trigger.

The moment you feel yourself wobble.

It shakes you loose from everything you thought you'd already mastered—not because you're failing, but because your system is recalibrating to hold more. It's not a step backward. It's not proof you're broken. It's the invitation to deepen into everything you've been practicing.

Because this is when the work gets real.

Not the kind you can jot down in a journal or revisit in a podcast. The lived work. The in-your-body, in-your-trigger, in-the-moment kind of work that doesn't wait until it's convenient. This is embodiment—not as a concept, but as a choice.

You've already done the unraveling. You've told the truth. You've traced the pattern to its root and met the version of you who learned to react that way. And yet, just because you've seen it doesn't mean you won't feel it again. Just because you've rewritten the belief doesn't mean your body doesn't still brace when it gets poked.

Healing isn't amnesia. It's remembering differently.

And this moment—the inconvenient one, the uncomfortable one, the one where everything in you wants to check out or shut down—isn't a test. It's a return. It's the moment you decide what happens next.

Because while you don't always get to choose what rises,you do get to choose who leads.

The old you who hustles to fix it?

The younger part who spirals to stay safe?

The people-pleaser who softens her truth to keep the peace?

Or the version of you who has done the work—and is ready to live it.

That's the choice point. Not flashy. Not loud. But powerful.

Because what you choose in *this* moment?

That's what rewires your future.

When Growth Isn't Glamorous

People love the highs of growth—the clarity, the break-throughs, the visceral yes that lands in your body when everything clicks into place. There's nothing like that momentum: your voice feels steady, your message aligned, your actions mirroring the future you've been working toward.

But expansion isn't measured in those highs. Not really.

It's not about how powerful you feel when everything is flowing. It's about who you are when it's not. The real growth happens in the quieter moments—the in-between spaces where the results haven't shown up yet, and your mind begins to question if the shift you made was real.

It's not always dramatic. Sometimes it's a launch that lands softer than expected. A piece of content that's met with silence. A conversation that didn't unfold the way you rehearsed it in your head. These are the spaces where your nervous system subtly asks, *"Do we really believe this new identity, or are we going back to what's familiar?"*

This isn't the glamorous part of growth. But it's where it counts the most.

Because when the old pattern resurfaces—when doubt creeps in and the old story pulls at you like gravity—that's when you find out if what you're building is rooted or simply rehearsed. Anyone can speak powerfully when momentum is high. Anyone can embody confidence when their external world is mirroring back their worth. But true expansion is measured in who you are when no one's watching. When the room is quiet. When the mirror reflects an old version of you asking to be believed again.

This is where most people misread the moment. They interpret the wobble as failure, the fear as regression, the trigger as proof the work didn't land. But that's not the truth. You're not breaking down—you're breaking in.

Breaking into a deeper level of self-trust. Into the version of you who no longer needs external confirmation to feel internal clarity. Into the grounded awareness that the reaction isn't a reason to spiral—it's a moment to return to presence and choose again.

Because that's what this space is really about—not bypassing the challenge or pretending it doesn't affect you, but choosing to meet it with more presence, more honesty, and more grounded power than ever before.

Integration doesn't happen in hindsight. It happens right here, in real time. It happens the moment you stop treating contraction as a crisis and start honoring it as a training ground.

Your Reaction Is a Signal, Not a Setback

It starts subtly.

An email that lands wrong. A look that tightens your chest. The silence that echoes a little too loudly, tugging at something unspoken inside of you. Your body reacts before your mind can catch up. You feel the spiral threaten to take hold—the urge to shut down, to over-explain, to retreat into the old ways that once kept you safe.

But this is where everything shifts—not because the reaction disappears, but because now, you know how to meet it.

This is what Code 3 whispers in these moments: your reaction is a signal. A flag. A thread leading back to something unresolved, not to be feared—but followed with compassion.

It's not proof that you're failing. It's a moment that asks, *Can you stay?*

Can you stay with the discomfort—without assigning it a meaning that makes you smaller?

Can you let the trigger speak—without letting it lead?

Will you choose to pause, even when your body wants to sprint toward the familiar?

Because the reaction itself isn't the problem. It's the story you're tempted to attach to it—the one that says,

See? Nothing's changed. You're not ready. You'll never get this right. That's the part that pulls you off track.

But you know better now.

You're not unraveling. You're integrating.

You're not back where you started. You're being given the opportunity to choose again—from power, not pattern.

This is where the Trigger Response Method™ becomes more than a tool—it becomes a practice. Not a fix, but a framework for presence. A way to pause in the middle of the moment, to feel what's rising, and to remember that who you are becoming is stronger than what's being reactivated.

You don't have to perform calm. You don't have to pretend it doesn't hurt. But you also don't have to collapse into it.

You get to stay centered. You get to choose your response.

You get to honor the signal without making it a sentence.

That's what makes this moment powerful.

Not the absence of reaction, but the presence of choice.

Setbacks Aren't Regression—They're Rewiring

The moment you stop chasing a version of success that's linear, polished, and forever rising, something inside you exhales. Because that version—no matter how compelling—was never the full story. It was a performance. One that left no room for nuance, no space for depth, no allowance for the real, often messy process of transformation.

Setbacks were never detours. They've always been part of the expansion. Data points that show you where your nervous system still flinches. Mirrors that reflect the stories still running in the background. Invitations not to undo the work—but to deepen it.

But most people never make it past this part. Not because they aren't capable. Not because they lack desire or vision. But because they misread the moment.

They feel a trigger and decide they must not be healed. They hit a plateau and assume something must be wrong. They have one hard day and question whether they're truly meant for this path. Discomfort gets mis-interpreted as disqualification.

But what if that's not the truth?

What if this is the part where your body learns to hold more—where your nervous system, your identity, your capacity all start stretching to meet the vision you've already declared? What if this tension, this pause, this pull back into the familiar… is actually the training ground?

Because expansion doesn't always feel like momentum. Sometimes, it feels like resistance. Sometimes it feels like standing in the middle of the old story with just enough self-awareness to know there's another option—and choosing it anyway, even before it feels natural.

That's the moment most people skip. They retreat. They wait until it feels easier, more certain, more validated.

But if you can stay in it—if you can meet the setback not as failure, but as feedback—something inside you begins to recalibrate. Not with drama. Not with fanfare. But with quiet, grounded power. A shift that starts from the inside and ripples outward.

Because this is where the work becomes embodied. This is where you stop performing your future—and start becoming it.

Integration Is the Quiet Revolution

Here's what most books won't tell you—what most personal growth paths forget to mention: you will have moments when you forget. You'll forget how far you've come. You'll forget how much you've already shifted. You'll forget that you are no longer your old patterns.

And that forgetting? It doesn't mean the work didn't work. It doesn't mean you've slipped backwards. It doesn't erase a single moment of growth. It simply invites a deeper question: how quickly can you remember?

Because this is what transformation really looks like—not in how flawlessly you move forward, but in how gently, how powerfully, you return. The space between reaction and awareness starts to collapse. The gap between contraction and clarity begins to narrow. The voice that once spiraled into stories now pauses—just long enough for you to choose again.

That's integration. Not loud. Not always obvious. But quietly potent.

This is where The Trigger Response Method™ becomes more than a method. It becomes embodied. It becomes lived. It becomes a part of who you are—not just something you remember when things fall apart.

It becomes your muscle memory. Not because you never wobble. But because you know how to find your way back. Faster. Softer. Truer.

And that? That's the real revolution.

What to Do When the Work Gets Loud

There comes a point where you don't need another reminder that patterns will rise. You already know that. You've done the work, you've walked through the fire, and you've seen your old stories up close.

So when the wobble hits, it's not about knowing more—it's about applying what you already know.

This is where The Trigger Response Method™ becomes your real-time tool. Not a theory you remember later, but a practice you reach for in the middle of the moment.

Here's how to move through it:

First, pause.

Interrupt the velocity of the story trying to sweep you away. You're not avoiding the emotion—you're creating space between it and your response.

Then name it.

"This is a reaction." "This is fear speaking through an old pattern." "This is my body trying to protect me from something it once didn't know how to hold."

You don't need to judge it. You don't need to fix it. You just need to acknowledge it—so it doesn't get to lead.

Now meet it with compassion.

Not coddling. Not bypassing.

But a grounded recognition that your system is showing you where safety still needs to be built.

This is TRM in the wild. Not just noticing the trigger, but staying with yourself through the heat of it. Letting the method bring you back into your body, your breath, your agency.

From here, ask better questions—not from panic, but from presence.

Not "Why is this happening again?"

But: "What is this moment revealing?" "What part of me still believes this pattern keeps me safe?" "What new truth is ready to be integrated right here?"

And then return to the Codes. Let them guide you home.

Code 1: Where am I outsourcing my power in this moment?

Code 2: What identity is behind this reaction?

Code 3: What is this trigger trying to reveal to me?

Code 4: How can I make it safe to hold what's here?

Code 5: Is there a truth I've been avoiding?

Code 6: What would choosing differently look like right now?

Code 7: How can I lead myself through this before anything else?

You don't need to journal for hours or wait until the emotion passes to shift.

You just need to stay conscious. Long enough to choose alignment over autopilot. Presence over pattern.

And then, when you feel grounded—take action. Not from panic or urgency. Not to fix or prove.

Just the next aligned move that honors where you are and who you're becoming.

That's what integration really looks like.

It's TRM in motion.

It's The Expansion Code™ embodied.

It's everything you've learned—lived.

Not just when things feel clear.

But when they don't. And you decide to lead anyway.

You're Not Falling Behind—You're Expanding Through It

This isn't a collapse. It's a strengthening.

Not proof that you're behind—but confirmation that you're becoming the kind of person who doesn't just understand alignment when things are clear, but lives it in the in-between. In the tension. In the moments no one sees.

You're not here to chase perfection. You're here to stay present enough to respond in a new way. That's the difference now. That's the edge you've earned.

Because you're no longer waiting to feel ready. You're not asking for conditions to be perfect. You're not outsourcing your capacity to what happens around you.

You're the one holding the pen.

You're the one regulating your posture—when the story gets loud, when the fear resurfaces, when the pattern flares.

And most importantly, you're the one holding the power.

This is what it looks like to expand for real. Not clean. Not curated. But embodied. And that's how you hold more. That's how you lead. That's how you build forward.

This is what it means to live the Expansion Code—not just when the light's green, but when the ground shakes.

You're not just surviving your setbacks anymore.

You're expanding through them.

Chapter Eleven

Welcome to the Embodiment Era

This isn't where the journey ends.

It's where it roots. Where everything you've awakened finally settles into the body. Into your breath. Into the way you speak to yourself when no one else can hear.

You're not chasing clarity anymore. You *are* the clarity.

You're no longer measuring your progress by how much you achieve or how fast you move—but by how deeply you're willing to meet yourself in the quiet.

This is the part no one glamorizes.

Where growth doesn't look like leaps and breakthroughs.

It looks like subtle shifts in your posture.

Like a softer voice in your head.

Like catching the spiral before it starts—and choosing to stay.

You've done the unraveling.

You've walked through the memories, the masks, the identities that once ran the show.

You've interrupted the loops. You've paused long enough to *see* them. To question what used to feel automatic.

You've stopped mistaking survival for strength. You've stopped calling your reactivity a personality trait.

You've learned to feel the tremble—and move anyway.

That's not just awareness. That's integration.

That's not just insight. That's embodiment.

You are no longer the woman who needs to perform to feel powerful.

You're no longer the version of you who needed the world to agree in order to feel valid.

What lives here now—beneath the old roles, the old proving, the old protection—is presence.

The kind that doesn't flinch when things feel uncertain.

The kind that knows the difference between urgency and truth.

The kind that doesn't need to broadcast transformation to trust that it's happening.

You've stopped asking the world to crown you.

Because you've already claimed the seat.

Your work now isn't to earn it. It's to *occupy* it fully.

You are not looking for the next secret, the next strategy, the next fix.

You're no longer seduced by shortcuts or obsessed with outcomes.

Because you understand: it's not about where you're going.

It's about *how* you're choosing to walk.

This is the arrival you didn't know you were working toward.

Not a peak moment. Not a finish line.

A homecoming.

To the power that was never outside of you.

To the voice that's no longer drowned out by performance.

To the version of you that doesn't shrink to belong,

doesn't dilute to be liked, and doesn't wait for external validation to move with conviction.

This is the woman who leads differently.

She doesn't hustle for worth.

She doesn't abandon herself to be chosen.

She doesn't build momentum off a foundation that requires her to disappear to succeed.

She leads with wholeness.

With quiet certainty.

With a truth that no longer needs to be shouted to be felt.

And the world feels her differently—because *she* feels herself differently.

You've rewritten the rules.

You've reclaimed the pen.

You've rebuilt your relationship with power, not as something to hold onto—but as something to *come home to*.

Now, the work is no longer about uncovering who you are.

It's about *living it*.

Without apology. Without the performance. Without the pressure to earn what you've always been worthy of.

This isn't where it ends.

This is where it finally begins to live in you.

You've Met the Codes. Now You Embody Them.

These Codes were never just clever lines to highlight or mantras to memorize.

They were never meant to live in a notebook, a workshop, or a caption.

They were always meant to live in *you*.

Not as rules.

As a rhythm.

Not as something you recite when things fall apart.

But something you return to when it matters most.

These are not tools to reach for—they're instincts you now move from.

They're not a framework. They're a *frequency*.

A way of being that doesn't just shift your outcomes... it rewires your origin point.

You're not checking off boxes anymore.

You're building your life from a completely different baseline.

You don't need to think about the Codes to remember them.

They show up in the way you *walk into the room now.*

In the breath you take before responding.

In the groundedness that rises when old chaos tries to pull you back.

Let's name them—again, not to teach you, but to *honor* the version of you who now lives them.

Code One lives in your stillness.

In the moment you stop outsourcing your authority and start remembering that your power never lived outside of you. Not in your clients. Not in your income. Not in your follower count. *You* are the source. And you finally believe it.

Code Two speaks when you no longer hustle for worth.

When you catch yourself reaching for the old pattern—and pause to ask: Who's making this decision? Is this my future identity or my past survival strategy? And when the answer's clear—you move accordingly.

Code Three shows up like a quiet guide in the heat of reactivity.

Where you once collapsed into the emotion, now you

lean in. You don't bypass the feeling. You hold it. You listen. And you lead yourself through—not out of pain, but through the pattern.

Code Four is why you're no longer flinching when ease enters the room.

Why you're no longer sabotaging the good. Why you can finally *receive*—rest, money, love, recognition—without shrinking or spinning out. Because you've taught your body that having more doesn't mean losing yourself.

Code Five rises with your integrity.

When the pressure to pretend shows up, you don't reach for the polished mask. You stay honest. You name what's real. And you let that truth lead, even if it makes people uncomfortable—because you're done abandoning yourself for someone else's comfort.

Code Six hums in the space between reaction and response.

The fork in the road where your system used to spiral. Now? You catch it. You breathe. You choose differently—not once, not perfectly—but over and over, until the choice becomes who you are.

Code Seven is the backbone.

It's in how you move when no one is clapping.

It's in the commitment you honor behind the scenes.

It's in the boundary you hold on the days it would be easier to fold.

Because you don't just lead others now.

You lead yourself first.

You're not practicing the Codes anymore.

You *are* the Code in motion.

The Codes Don't Just Live in You—They Lead You.

You don't carry these Codes in your mind like reminders.

You embody them now—in the pause before the pattern,

in the breath between reaction and response,

in the choices no one sees but you feel all the way through.

This isn't something you access when things feel calm.

It's what anchors you when they don't.

It's the instinct that kicks in the moment fear rises.

Not to bypass it. But to *meet it.*

To stay rooted when your old wiring tells you to run.

To remember who you are when your nervous system tries to forget.

Because this is the difference now:

The Codes aren't something you have to go looking for.

They *rise* in the moment you need them most.

They live in your spine when you set a boundary.

In your voice when you speak the hard truth.

In your silence when you choose not to defend.

In your pace when you no longer chase.

You carry them in how you move through resistance.

In how you stay with yourself when discomfort hits.

In how you recalibrate to clarity after chaos tries to cloud your path.

Because embodiment isn't just a feeling—it's a *way of being*.

The Expansion Code™ was never about adding more to who you are.

It was about *coming home to yourself.*

It was about clearing the noise.

Undoing the performance.

And remembering the quiet, unshakable knowing underneath it all.

You don't lead from fear anymore.

You don't bend for validation.

You don't chase worth like it lives anywhere outside of you.

Now, you lead from truth.

From clarity.

From wholeness.

And when you forget—which you will—you won't stay lost for long.

You won't spiral the same way.

You won't collapse like you used to.

You'll notice faster.

You'll return sooner.

You'll anchor deeper.

Because now?

The Codes don't just live in you.

They lead you.

And you trust yourself enough to follow.

Let This Be Your Line in the Sand

This work was never about becoming someone new.

It was about coming back to the version of you who always knew.

The version who felt clear before the world made her second-guess.

Who moved boldly before she learned to shrink.

Who trusted herself before she was taught to perform.

She wasn't lost.

She was waiting.

And now—you've found your way back.

You've remembered her voice. Her rhythm. Her power. And you've expanded her into someone even deeper, even more rooted, even more unapologetically whole.

So don't rush past this moment.

Don't dismiss the shift just because it wasn't loud.

There's power in the subtle.

There's impact in what no one else can see but you can feel all the way through.

You don't need a new to-do list right now.

You don't need to map out a perfect plan for what's next. What you need is to meet the version of you who made it here—and name what changes because of it.

Let this be your threshold.

The before and after.

The place where you stop performing expansion and start living it.

The moment you stop waiting for clarity and decide to become it.

This isn't about writing the perfect paragraph.

It's about choosing a new baseline.

It's about no longer delaying your embodiment until the conditions feel ideal.

It's about leading from the version of you who already is.

So take your time.

Feel the weight of this moment.

Let it settle into your body, your breath, your bones.

Because you don't need to earn your arrival.

You just need to live from it.

This is where you begin again—on your terms, in your rhythm, with your truth at the center.

Not because the work is over—

But because you've finally remembered:

You were always the one.

Chapter Twelve

The Living, Breathing Expansion Code™ Manifesto

*T*his is where it becomes yours.
Not just a book you read, but a rhythm you live.

The Living, Breathing Expansion Code™ Manifesto

I no longer chase what was never mine.

I no longer shrink to make others comfortable.

I no longer need proof to trust myself.

I honor my triggers as teachers.

I meet my reactions with curiosity, not shame.

I lead myself first—especially when it's inconvenient.

I choose to build safety within, Speak truth without apology, And return to alignment when I forget.

I am no longer available for old stories that dim my power.

I am no longer waiting for clarity to act.

I am no longer confusing contraction with failure.

I lead from identity, not urgency.

I rise with integrity, not perfection.

I expand not to impress—but to live fully expressed.

The Codes are no longer something I study.

They are something I *live.*

This is not a chapter I close.

This is the life I open.

And I'm ready.

Chapter Thirteen

Integration Toolkit

Your Quick-Reference to the TRM + Expansion Code™

The Trigger Response Method™ (TRM)

*T*he five steps to shift in real time—so your reaction doesn't run your results.

Step 1: Recognize the Trigger

Catch the moment your body tightens, your breath shortens, or your mind spirals—this is your cue to pause.

Step 2: Observe & Understand

Instead of reacting, witness what's rising. Ask: *"What is this really about?"*

Step 3: Identify the Payoff

Every pattern serves a purpose. Find the hidden safety it's been giving you.

Step 4: Pause at the Choice Point

This is your moment of power. Breathe, get present, and choose who you want to be in this moment.

Step 5: Choose Your Aligned Response

Lead yourself forward—not from fear, but from the truth of who you're becoming.

The Expansion Code™

Seven truths to live by. Let them guide you back to your power when the noise creeps in.

Code 1: Your Power Is Internal

It was never outside of you. It doesn't need to be earned, proved, or performed—it only needs to be remembered.

Code 2: Identity Drives Everything

You don't rise beyond who you believe you are. Shift your self-concept, and your entire reality shifts with it.

Code 3: Your Reaction Is the Signal

Triggers aren't setbacks—they're invitations. Notice the reaction, follow it to the root, and lead yourself through it.

Code 4: Make It Safe to Hold More

You don't sabotage success—you protect yourself from what your body doesn't yet feel safe to receive. Rewire that safety.

Code 5: Tell the Truth

Growth begins with radical honesty. Name what you want. Own what's in the way. Lead from what's real.

Code 6: Choose Differently

Every moment offers a Choice Point. Power lives in the

pause—where you respond as who you're becoming, not who you've been.

Code 7: Lead Yourself First

You don't need a crowd to start leading. Show up in integrity behind the scenes. The world will feel it.

Daily Expansion Anchors

Use these as mantras, reminders, or energetic anchors throughout your day.

- I don't need to prove what I already am.

- This is a trigger, not a truth.

- I choose alignment over urgency.

- I lead from who I'm becoming—not who I've been.

- I am safe to hold more.

- My power is internal—and I already have access to it.

- I don't abandon myself for comfort or approval.

- I trust myself to respond differently this time.

- I don't spiral. I return.

- I don't chase ease—I build it from within.

- My identity sets the tone. My actions follow her lead.

- This moment is a Choice Point. I get to decide who I am.

Integration Prompts

Use these questions to self-coach and deepen the embodiment of this work.

- What am I reacting to—and what might this really be about?

- What version of me is leading right now?

- Is this discomfort actually unsafe—or just unfamiliar?

- Where am I still waiting for permission instead of choosing alignment?

- What pattern wants to run the show—and what would I choose instead?

- If I were already the next-level version of me... how would I respond?

- Where am I outsourcing power I could return to myself today?

- What is this moment asking me to remember?

- What emotional payoff have I been unconsciously choosing?

- What part of me still believes I can't hold this—and how can I show her she's safe?

About the author

Kayla Burch is a globally recognized expert in subconscious reprogramming, emotional leadership, and identity expansion. She is the founder of the internationally renowned **Coaching Mastery Certification**, and the creator of two groundbreaking frameworks that have transformed the personal development and coaching industry: **The Trigger Response Method™** and **The Expansion Code™**.

With a signature blend of deep emotional wisdom and practical integration, Kayla is known for helping high-achievers break free from invisible ceilings, emotional reactivity, and old identities that no longer fit—so they can lead, build, and live from their fullest expression.

Her journey began in the trenches of overachievement, perfectionism, and quiet burnout. What looked like success on the outside often came at the cost of inner peace. Until she realized: the real transformation isn't about what you do—it's about who you *become while doing it*. That revelation became the foundation for her body of work.

Today, Kayla's teachings are sought after by leaders, coaches, and entrepreneurs around the world who are ready to build lives and businesses rooted in clarity, safety, power, and truth. Through her best-selling programs, high-level mentorship, and sold-out masterclasses, she has helped thousands activate their next level—not by hustling harder, but by healing deeper.

Her work doesn't just inspire change.

It creates the kind of transformation that lasts.

You can explore more of Kayla's world at **www.kayl aburch.com**